MIND
OVER
MATTER

MIND OVER MATTER

Higher Martial Arts

SHI MING
with **Siao Weijia**

Translated by
Thomas Cleary

Frog, Ltd.
Berkeley, California

Mind Over Matter: Higher Martial Arts

Published by Frog, Ltd.

Frog, Ltd. books are distributed by
North Atlantic Books
P.O. Box 12327
Berkeley, California 94701

Cover photos of Shi Ming by Siao Weijia
Photo of Siao Weijia by Eva Siao
Cover calligraphy by Jin-Duan Lin
Cover and book design by Paula Morrison
Typeset by Catherine Campaigne
Printed in the United States of America by Malloy Lithographing

First Frog, Ltd. publication 1994

Library of Congress Cataloging-in-Publication Data
Shi, Ming
    Mind over matter : higher martial arts / Shi Ming and Siao Weijia :
    translated by Thomas Cleary.
        p.   cm.
    Translated from Chinese.
    ISBN 1-883319-15-3
    1. Martial arts—Psychological aspects.   I. Siao, Weijia.
II. Title.
GV1102.7.P75S55   1994
796.8—dc20   93-40427
                                                                   CIP

        3   4   5   6   7   8   9 / 98   97   96   95

CONTENTS

TRANSLATOR'S FOREWORD

In his acclaimed series *Healing and the Mind,* Bill Moyers introduced America to Shi Ming, reputed to be one of the leading masters of martial arts in China. Shi Ming's astounding demonstrations of *jin,* the unique inner power developed by advanced martial artists, brought Moyers face to face with the perennial dilemma of science; even as science seeks to confirm its results, it must also continue to seek knowledge of the unknown in order to fulfill its original nature and mission.

In his *Farewell to Reason,* Paul Feyerabend, the distinguished and controversial historian of science, places the dilemma of Western science in a universalistic perspective: "Cultural variety cannot be tamed by a formal notion of objective truth because it contains a variety of such notions. Those who insist on a particular formal notion are just as liable to run into problems (in their sense) as the defenders of a particular conception of the world."* Compare this to the opening statement of *Tao Te Ching,* the classic of Taoism: "A way that can be expressed is not an eternal Way."

Feyerabend continues: "Who would have thought that the boundary between subject and object would be questioned as part of a scientific argument and that science would be advanced thereby? Yet this was, precisely what happened in the quantum theory, in physiological studies such as those of Maturana and Varela (and earlier, in Mach's investigations on the physiology of perception.)." (ibid.) Systematic questioning and transcending of the boundary between subject and object, acknowledged to have resulted in such breakthroughs in Western science, is in fact one of the bases of traditional

---

*Feyerabend, *Farewell to Reason* (London/NewYork, Verso, 1987), p. 9

Chinese science, which has also made breakthroughs in energy and perception in that way. This unique book by Master Shi Ming and his disciple Siao Weija calls upon both traditional and modern concepts to explain the extraordinary developments of mind and body produced by the science of higher Chinese martial arts.

New Perspectives on Martial Arts

by Siao Weijia, Li Jianmin, and Yu Gongbao

THE RAPID DEVELOPMENT of modern civilization and technology has brought people into a domain formerly only imagined; human beings ride rockets to the moon, countless robots and machines have taken the place of heavy labor. Self-regulated and automated production lines are gradually freeing people from simplex tasks that not only tire them out but also make them subordinate to machinery. Computers are replacing or reducing the use of the human brain in every field.

But just as humanity is becoming complacent about conquering nature, and is continuing endless consumption and ceaseless ambition, all sorts of perils and dangers are unexpectedly also confronting humanity, entrapping this world of actualities, which sometimes cannot avoid losing direction through blindness. Destruction of balance in the biosphere, the threat of nuclear devastation, pollution of the environment, depletion of resources, economic arrhythmia, psychological aberrations and new ills of the age — at this point intoxication turns into anxiety, and the hangover induces a rude awakening and self-examination.

Conquest must touch off counterconquest. With each step of human conquest over nature, we encounter the reaction of the equilibrating power of nature. This is the principle that whatever comes to a climax must reverse; everyone recognizes this fact. The central issue of the world of the future is how to attune the relationship between the individual, society, and nature, how to transform a war of conquest into a harmonious, united collaboration of humanity and nature. Being a combined product of nature and society, human-kind will be at the center of the issue.

There is a real problem confronting humankind and modern science, one that cannot be overlooked. Science is a product of economic development, and it also serves the development of an economy, to the point where even if finance began with human needs, it does not work only for the benefit of humanity, not entirely as people imagine. Finance is animated by its own rules; not only is it often alienated from, or contradictory to, urgent human needs, it also continues to create new demands that people originally did not have, demands that are not of use to their complete development, and which can even influence their progress and evolution along a misguided path to self-loss and self-destruction.

Very few people consider our central purpose to be a gradual surrender and deterioration under the cover of all sorts of complicated systems of fancy scientific and economic terminology, to the point where many primary capacities and skills lapse from a manifest state into latency because of having been replaced by technology. This devolutionary tendency cannot but be called a big mistake.

Science causes people a rude awakening, when we realize that humanity in a civilized state has already lost something, and is thus in urgent need of replenishment. We reflect that there have been various gaps and limitations in purposes and methods ever since science has been dominant, urgently calling for the actualization of a new breakthrough, a new leap of progress.

Human needs as they are undistorted and undeflected by commercial economics, latent human capacities and a more reasonable relationship between humanity and nature, the elevation of the level of development of the human race itself as well as the overall development of health—such issues as these have aroused the sincere concern and attention of the entire scientific and intellectual community. With the economies and technologies of newly developing nations of the East catching up to the developed modern West, and the developed nations of the West turning to the ancient civilizations of the East to search out their roots, this concern and attention have fostered an ever deepening dialogue and intercourse between each field of study, between East and West, between the present and the past, between macrocosmic and microcosmic views, using scientific thinking freely to nurture a new creative attitude and scientific methodology, facilitating communion between past and present, East and West, such that they interpenetrate and complement each other.

In scientific information theory, robotics, systematics, and entropics, the highest achievements of cosmophysics and particle physics, and ancient Eastern "mysticism," the philosophy of nature as an organic whole in which Nature and humanity are united, and the idea of universal laws governing the totality of the universe, call and respond to each other over vast distances, knocking on the door of postindustrial society. The sails of life science based on the satisfaction of authentic and long-term human needs are slowly rising, announcing to science and humanity the coming of a new era.

The legacy of corruption in traditional Chinese culture is one of the main culprits in the general deterioration and backwardness of the Chinese nation and people over the last few centuries, and is being subjected to ever greater, deeper, and sharper criticism. This criticism is for the sake of a great liberation, a great revolution, to catch up with the developed nations of the world, to participate in the world market, to modernize the society, polity, and economy of China. In short, to revitalize China and sweep away a millennium's barriers of thought by getting rid of the stale and the rotten, to open up new consciousness and new thinking, it is necessary to be about the business of revolutionizing the spiritual aspect of our people.

Nevertheless, even in times of most intensive forward movement, the finest product of traditional Chinese culture, its ever youthful essence, has never ceased its own work of discovery, perpetuation, and expression, regardless of misunderstanding, destruction, or oppression. Countless people of knowledge and perception who have penetrated deeply into the underlying currents of history, who have found a treasure that will ever shine forth with a brilliant light for humankind, who have been silent and unknown yet indefatigable, having at heart an ever fresh enthusiasm, combining related scientific results, have never given up intensive research. After the Revolution and Liberation, within the short period of ten years there appeared innumerable sprouts of scientific research, which have nearly blossomed into full flower.

When the fruits of the technological civilization of a developed country are clearly showing various signs of decadence, when the law of competition has fully exposed the various kinds of imbalance it brings to nature, society, and the individual, when physical and mental injuries have left their aftereffects, people at least generally realize that competition also requires compensation and balance. Such effective compensation and balance, furthermore, can be found in the ancient culture of the East, especially China, which seeks the highest spiritual state, seeking dynamic balance in all activity and movement. Thus the essence of traditional Chinese culture, much like a newly unearthed artifact, has been rediscovered by human civilization.

Discovery is not the same as mastery. What was already a fertile field for the people of olden times is for people of modern times still virgin ground requiring intensive cultivation, fertilization, and irrigation. As far as research into ancient Chinese civilization is concerned, while some minor results have of course been obtained, nevertheless on the whole it has been a series of failures, making people aware that there is still within Eastern culture an extraordinarily effective scientific system that cannot be simply explained, interpreted, or accepted by modern science. So a new way out must be found. Traditional philosophy, medicine, hygiene, and physical education are all facing the same kind of problem.

In such a profound and far-reaching interaction between scientific culture and social thinking, Chinese martial arts have also beautifully set forth their tremendous fascination, seeming to show unlimited presence without even intending it, and giving ever greater demonstrations of their irreplaceable function.

In traditional Chinese culture, martial arts constitute a priceless treasure, and a science with a vast experiential background. The many styles and forms of martial arts, and the nearly mystical individual experiences they bring, have fascinated people everywhere; their incomparable profound inner contents have inspired deep reflection in people everywhere, and their lofty realms of experience often make people feel they can only be longed for but never actually reached. Thus, like all pristine yet profound truths, they have caused people to become so involved that many have gone to infinite pains in their quest. Yet very few people have attained the mysterious realm of great awakening in which everything is comprehended through one realization, and after attaining which no effort at all is expended.

Their extraordinary character and transcendental physical and mental contents have unavoidably caused martial arts to be subject to misunderstanding and attack throughout history by ordinary people with vulgar opinions, and have suffered both man-made and natural oppression. At the same time, the theories, practices, and individual techniques and peak spiritual experiences that have gone through countless refinements along this tortuous and perilous road have not failed to bring along the essence of ineffable wisdom that conceals infinite levels of deeper and deeper realization within layer after layer of masks of self-defense.

Nowadays, there are some people who reject martial arts as being "unprovable individual mystical experience," while there are others who praise martial arts as being the "crystallization of transcendental reason." Both of these opinions actually reflect the fact that advanced martial arts training produces extraordinary physical and mental elements that give people a sense of unfathomable profundity, and martial arts have a deeply hidden value that cannot be comprehended at a glance.

People of the modern day have often been amazed at the cultural achievements of the ancient Chinese people; but they have also often been stymied by the thinking methods and the cryptic symbolic language of the ancients. The reception of martial arts has certainly been no exception to this. The scientific democratization trend of the May Fourth movement prompted a few martial artists with a grasp of the new culture and new science to look at martial arts from a new angle, attempting to use scientific language to decipher the symbolic codes of martial arts, and to make modern philosophical interpretations of classical theories. In the chaos and turmoil of the time, however, the Chinese people had plunged the energy of the nation, and indeed their whole lives, into a decisive battle to rescue the Chinese nation and people from a devastating fate. Under these conditions, in such an era, early attempts at scientific study of martial arts certainly had no power to obtain outstanding results.

During the 1950s and 1960s, the young People's Republic of China rose from the ruins. While healing the wounds of war, the thoughts of the people turned to a peaceful, constructive life. Now the martial arts were widely promoted as physical culture, as exercises to strengthen the body. And yet, because there was no call for non-military and nonpolice personnel to practice aggressive and defensive pugilistic exercise, this nearly brought about the loss of the inner work of martial arts, the truly extraordinary technical patterns, including the corresponding unique exercises and secret methods, as well as the core inner content. Scientific study of martial arts was limited to the domains of exercise routines and physical therapy.

Coming to the beginning of the 1980s, having gone through ten years of turmoil, a wounded People's Republic of China absorbed the lessons of various mistakes, stood up straight, and went on a new path of complete modernization. At this time, martial arts finally began to revive again, bringing their total value with them. Striding quickly out the door to the enthusiasm of the Chinese people and the applause of international appreciation, bounding onto the silver screen transcending national borders, Chinese martial arts have reached the five continents of earth.

Everywhere throughout China, popular types of pugilism have set off a profusion of martial arts studios and martial arts teams. Even the institutes of higher learning have established their own martial arts teams. Martial arts have begun to permeate the Chinese people's physical education system, and China has organized contests on the prefectural, city, and national levels. There have already been many international martial arts contests, and there is a growing momentum toward making martial arts an Olympic event.

This rapid development and expansion have promoted overall dissemination and improvement of martial arts exercise. They have also promoted entirely new scientific research in martial arts. Martial arts have found their way into popular study groups, institutes of higher learning, and national research institutes. The Chinese government has organized large-scale, nationwide efforts to unearth and systematize the heritage of martial arts; it has also set up the Chinese Martial Arts Research Institute. Scientists, researchers, university students, the literary and art worlds, and the world of philosophy have combined their own specialists' knowledge of modern technology, publishing research articles and scientific hypotheses in martial arts magazines at all levels. The intercommunication of martial arts and science has developed into an independent trend.

In June and July of 1987, the first national conference on scientific study of martial arts was held in Beijing under the auspices of the National Committee on Physical Education, the People's Physical Culture Publishing Company, the Chinese Martial Arts Research Institute, and Chinese martial arts magazines, involving units from every level of the national structure. At this conference, which was organized on an unprecedented scale, mass high level contact and full interaction took place for the first time between researchers in every field of modern science and the martial arts education and training going on in the provinces, towns, and specialist institutions.

Another result of this conference was the establishment of a national learned society for the scientific study of martial arts. This society links the scientists researching martial arts with workers in martial arts at all levels, local martial artists, and fans of martial arts, in the form of a nationwide organization. Thus, a new flower has opened in the blooming garden of modern science, a new domain of scientific research.

Even if the scope, depth, accuracy, and specialization of the discussion still await some improvement, even if the essence of martial arts still awaits more penetrating discovery and organization for a more thorough development and sublimation, and even though martial arts organizations also need better and more natural systems, nevertheless the historical significance of this conference far transcends the initial academic results and the joy of the participants. It showed that martial arts have won the attention of the nation and society at all levels, that the originally indivisible processes of martial arts and science have started to reconverge, and are beginning to carry on effective dialogue and cooperation, representing the birth of a new science. All of this foreshadows the arrival of a new era, a new age, in which Chinese martial arts will be modernized, integrated with science and society on a large scale. Therefore, this conference is a new landmark in the millennium-long history of the development of martial arts.

The authors of this book maintain that martial arts are distinct from any other system of physical exercise or self-defense, having extremely pronounced special characteristics. It is precisely these special characteristics that make it possible for martial arts to constitute a new, independent field of scientific inquiry, which is the motive and reason for writing this book. The following is a summary of some of these special characteristics.

The most essential, most outstanding, and most profound peculiarity of martial arts, especially higher martial arts, is their connection with philosophy, even when treated as a method of self-defense. Furthermore, because classical Chinese philosophy holds a holistic view of the universe in which all things have the same source, therefore martial arts also have an intimate relationship of mutual influence and interpenetration with every aspect of Chinese culture, including arts, sciences, and medicine.

Because of this, martial arts have not only brought fresh popular culture and psychological color; based on self-defense techniques, they have demonstrated a series of astonishing breakthroughs, with amazingly rapid progress. The martial arts originated from the basic instincts of self-defense and attack, went through a history of creating fighting methods, then passed into the domain of hygiene and physical exercise; in their heyday, they gained the depth and inner content of philosophy, as well as a holistic interrelationship with all domains of nature and human society. When advanced martial artists of the past announced that fighting technique per se is a minor art, this also made it known that martial arts had been sublimated from fighting into a way of seeking the Tao.

We need not discuss the nuances of the word "Tao," because in the philosophy of the ancients, the word "Tao" is just another name for "Truth," although with a somewhat richer and deeper sense than ordinarily understood. The word "Tao" also includes the meaning of "a path by which to seek truth." Thus "seeking the Tao" can be understood as the effort to seek truth. Seeking truth and producing happiness for humankind, furthermore, are the essence of all science and culture.

The concepts and terminology of Taoist, Confucian, and Buddhist philosophies can now be gradually decoded and interpreted to yield these same principles. The sublimation of martial arts from its primitive motives and purposes to the attainment of these philosophical teachings has assured that martial arts are no longer merely fighting techniques or physical culture, but are rather a psycho-physical activity in which classical Chinese philosophy, science, culture, and arts are combined into one. Based on this, the meaning of martial arts far transcends the domains of ordinary physical and mental exercises, or combative exercises. We can say that the highest level of martial arts is the philosophy of psychophysical enlightenment, while all other levels are graduated manifestations of different levels of philosophy.

Another breakthrough and leap forward made by martial arts as a way of self-defense is in placing the highest elevation of human character, virtue, and spiritual state far above mere attack and defense techniques. This has caused the fighting instinct, technology, and consciousness to be included in a broader, more lofty, and more appealing domain. In order to communicate this vast universe, advanced martial artists have not been satisfied with physical and mental health and strength, or with killing power and strategic skill. Because the violence of the elementary and middle levels of martial arts training shut off the finest and best of what could be hoped for, advanced martial artists gradually developed training conforming to medical principles and peaceful means of deciding superiority, making sure that once people had mastered the highest technical principles and fighting skills, they would not abandon the effort to seek the Tao and sublimate human character.

Chinese philosophy and humanistic ethics have a strong color of search for universal beauty and a fresh new aesthetic, rich in the special charm of folk art. This is also a major feature indispensable to martial arts. The many exercise routines of the various individual schools all have the same aesthetic standard of unification of form and spirit, with each one constituting a system. All of them have a quiet joyfulness, a formless color; all of them have a musical rhythm and meter, crescendo and diminuendo of mood, mixing and alternation of movement and stillness. The shapes formed by the human body, some firm, some soft, are like a rock carving, like floating clouds and flowing water, like inspiring poetry and art. There are an enormous number of lively and expressive movements and gestures imitating the movements of life: there is human body language expressing the cycles and energies of mountains and rivers, plants and trees, sun, moon, stars, and planets; there is symbolic language representing struggle and harmony between humanity and nature, and between people; there is also the human body's own capacity to intimate all sorts of subtle feelings and aesthetic senses of spirit and temperament. The ability of the esthetics of martial arts to express eternal life is a result of the interpenetration of martial arts and technology, philosophy, literature and art, music and painting, drama and dance.

"Nearby, find it in yourself; at a distance, find it in things." Every domain and branch of Chinese culture draws limitless nourishment and power from the vast universe outside oneself, from nature, society, and culture. Because of this, just as masters of Chinese painting emphasize the idea that "the effect is outside the brush," in higher martial arts as well, the craft is in the body but the effect is outside the fist.

The above noted peculiarities of martial arts, as well as the manifestation of self-transcendence, are inseparable from the breakthroughs made in technique and theory. Without fighting techniques, martial arts would no longer be martial arts; and yet the technical and theoretical aspects of pugilism are still based on biology, psychology, medical science, and dynamics. In particular, the combination of philosophy and dynamics has produced a key function.

As distinct from other exercise systems, martial arts make a particular point of mutual correspondence between inside and outside, the union of form and spirit, guided by the holistic view of the communion and union of Nature and humanity. This means that inner and outer exercises are practiced simultaneously (what is called the twin cultivation of essence and life). Furthermore, they form a training process in which emphasis on external work gradually gives way to emphasis on internal work.

In martial arts science, there is still no clear conceptual definition of inside and outside, but two major levels are generally recognized: in one sense, the inside is the mind or spirit, while the outside is the body or form; on another level, inside is the person, outside is the universe. (There are still many more deeper and more multifaceted distinctions.) Martial arts require people to refine the mind, refine the body, and refine energy. Inner work is refinement of the individual person, while outer work is the cultivation of the human capacity to commune responsively with the universe. In reality, it is a matter of mutual refinement of body and mind; the key is in the inner work, which is the energetics of martial arts, plus the corresponding mental exercises.

When all is said and done, the origin, core, and highest level of the inner and outer work of martial arts are all in refinement of mind. The basic principle of the training, that inside and outside join, enables people to gradually attain intercourse and merging of the totality of body and mind. The special training of consciousness and the respiratory system, gradually advancing, effectively regulates every system of the mechanical body as well as the technical capacities of the whole being; it regulates the entire nervous system and endocrine system, and at the same time gradually leads to a higher level of harmony and integration of the self with the external world (including both nature and society). Furthermore, the results of the basic principle of martial arts have provided present and future studies of the human body and human society with countless topics awaiting exploration and research.

The work of conjoining the internal and the external in a manner that conforms to philosophical and medical principle is capable of uncovering and tuning latent human capacities, and can also produce a supraordinary physical and mental constitution. Included therein are special processing by biodynamic techniques, special modes of thought, special conditions of health maintenance and life extension, and special epistemology and methodology.

Martial arts have not discovered any new principles of dynamics; but they have made amazing breakthroughs by developing the latent capacities of the body and brain on the basis of the principles of applied biodynamics. Martial arts emphasize the dynamic effects and training of firmness and flexibility, emptiness and fullness, movement and stillness, speed and slowness, and so on. They also pursue the physiological and psychological goal of higher cooperation and coordination of mind, spirit, will, energy, and the body. Many movements imitating life reflect the quest of martial arts to learn from the movements, morphologies, temperaments, and spiritual conditions of animals and plants, as well as from all sorts of dynamic phenomena in nature, how to restore, enrich, and fully attune our own pristine biodynamic and biological abilities, which we once had but have lost and never rediscovered.

The terminologies relating to the simple postures and complex routines of virtually all schools of martial arts are full of names imitating life. The simple postures are the so-called three doors known as the absolute, giving form to consciousness, and the eight trigrams. The twelve (animal) forms, thirteen alchemical methods, and so on, are called dragon and wind, falcon and snake, tiger and leopard, the bear, rooster and crane, the wild horse, the monkey, the lion, the wild cat, the sparrow, the sparrowhawk, the camel, the fish that burrows in the sand, and so on. There are also the meteor, the sun and moon, clouds and rain, wind and thunder, mountains and rivers, pine and cedar, clear spring and deep pond, ancient bell and horse crop, and so on and so forth. One could go on naming such terms endlessly.

Of course, martial arts certainly do not require people to return to a primitive, uncivilized, or even bestial state; rather, they take the restored and enriched instincts and latent capacities and elevate them to the highest level of consciousness. That is, martial arts carry out a comprehensive processing of instinct, the subconsciousness, and manifest consciousness. Because of this, the purpose of imitating life is to use forms to refine consciousness, use consciousness to refine inner power, and use inner power to refine the mind and spirit, in search of pervasive integration; it is a type of biodynamic principle and technology for seeking the highest level of integration through returning all things to their root.

Inner power (and energy) are concepts of physical and mental capacity and strength peculiar to martial arts. It can also be said that inner power is muscular strength that has been refined by special martial arts training, as well as its special mode of conduction. Inner power develops from crudeness and turbulence to fineness, lightness, and clarity; it develops from lever-like conduction to penetrating conduction, to traveling so that it is conducted to another body, to conduction outside the bodies of both oneself and one's adversary. When energy collects, it is inner power; when inner power disperses, it is energy: this enables the dynamic structure of the human body-mind to go from a solid state to a liquid state to a gaseous state, even to a field state, as well as a condition in which these various states interchange and complement each other, forming all sorts of combinations. These progressive breakthroughs exponentially expand the range of dynamic function of the human body, the latent capacity for technical processing, and the efficiency of fighting technique.

Martial arts and energetics are inseparable; the inner work of energetics is a core speciality of martial arts. We can say that the inner work of martial arts is energetics converted to martial arts. In essence, energetics are the technical foundation of martial arts, and are also the medical principles of martial arts. Thus the entire range of principle and theory of Chinese medicine, as refracted by energetics, also constitute a special feature of martial arts. Besides the normal hygienic safeguards promoted by Chinese medicine, Chinese medical standards of health and longevity characteristic of the ancient "realized people" in particular constitute a reliable basis for medical theories that have produced many long-tested and proven special effects. These include the theory of sensitive interaction between humanity and Nature, and the union of body and spirit; the theory of the energy channels, inner organs, and biological clock; and the special medical principles and psychophysical effects produced after the combining of martial arts and energetics. While they cure illness, they also strengthen the body; while they are technical principles of fighting, they also lengthen the life span. While they follow nature to extend life, they also oppose nature to renew life; while they involve a total development of health, they also disinter supranormal latent capacities.

Thus, medical science and energetics combined with and digested by martial arts are an inexhaustible source of all sorts of future research topics relating to the inner mysteries of life.

Medical science and martial arts are natural-born companions; many medical doctors are themselves great martial artists or masters of energetics, and many martial artists and energetics masters have also become medical doctors. At the advanced levels, medicine and martial arts are indivisible; the two are conjoined into one. Humankind will always require movement, and will always require health. So it goes without saying that movement and health are two perennial issues in the sciences of the human body. Because they attune and develop the total relationship between the human body and mind, martial arts also partake of the eternal force of life itself.

Quite evidently, the psychological training of martial arts on this level cannot but far transcend the boundaries and methods of any known psychological training. We need not even mention the technical patterns of the complete routines: simple postures are the starting point of the unification of martial arts and energetics, as well as a graduated technique for people to enter into stillness. Thus the simple postures already require people to go through principles and training analogous to what Buddhists call discipline, concentration, and insight, until people reach the state of profound stillness known to Buddhists as "emptiness," to Taoists as "noncontrivance," and to Confucians as "the infinite."

People are further required to bring this "stillness" to a high degree of resistance, such that it is stable and cannot be broken down. This not only has an effect on martial arts fighting technique whose value cannot be overestimated; it is also an unusually effective remedy for psychological illnesses. What is more, this profound stillness is the starting point and cornerstone of epistemology and methodology in Eastern philosophy; and in the path of martial arts, it is a necessary route to the ultimate attainment of the sudden enlightenment by which the pattern of all things is realized.

It is hardly to be wondered that a famous Nobel Prize-winning scientist from England considered sudden enlightenment to be a consciousness field not subject to disturbance, which consequently allows intrinsic intelligence to emerge. He also declared that the way out for bioscience in the future lies in the meditation techniques of the East.

Furthermore, the special characteristics and training noted earlier are at the same time also supranormal psychological training. This is why the term "refinement of consciousness" as we use it includes the essence and core of martial arts.

Movement and stillness produce each other; this is a unifying rule of the movement of heaven, earth, and the universe. Martial arts seek to coordinate human physical and mental capacities of movement with the order of the universe to the greatest possible degree. This is undoubtedly a special development of the latent capacities of the human body and brain, leading the physical and mental constitution to a supraordinary level.

An example of this is the martial arts emphasis on refinement of consciousness, and the principle of going through refinement of consciousness to the point where will is used in place of physical strength. This has already become a standard rule passed on generation to generation; it is also a top class special feature distinguishing martial arts from other fighting techniques. The final aim of this training is the unification of Nature and humanity; its mysterious, unfathomable inner principles have never yet been decoded by science.

Following the lead of martial arts theory and practice, we can recognize that the concept of "consciousness" does not refer to the abstract consciousness as ordinarily misconstrued by people, but to a condition in which body and mind are fused, spirit and matter are united. Here, "energy" is the capacity and the format through which inside and outside commune and become unified. Based on this, the present work boldly presents a new concept for a scientific hypothesis, that of consciousness being identical to dynamic thought, attempting to use this to interpret the mystic doctrine of using will rather than strength. This should also, furthermore, be considered a core characteristic of the whole constitution of martial arts.

Dynamic thought, as the name implies, is conscious thought rather than motor activity, but it also has a very powerful yet subtle biodynamic effect, which makes it clear that it is a result of a special attunement of muscular capacity and other biological and psychological capacities. Beyond this, dynamic thought (which is "consciousness") is a bridge to higher realms of martial arts technical principles and spiritual experience. The higher realms, moreover, (such as "will without conscious intent") also represent physical and mental apperception of a high order; this is the crystallization of thousands of years of philosophy in the brain of martial artists. Only with higher apperception is it possible to actualize the goal of uniting Nature and humanity.

The psychophysical peculiarity of martial arts referred to as "movement within taking shape outside" unfolds into the movements of the many types of martial arts boxing and paraphernalia routines, as well as countless variations of striking maneuvers. Using simple postures, long routines, and striking maneuvers, having practiced the basic exercises and trained the physical and mental constitution, one also practices advanced fighting arts. Each school of martial arts concentrates its exercise principles and methods into a comparatively small range of defined movements, and by going through them over and over, practicing countless times, they discover the methods of the best technical patterns; this too is an unusually fresh characteristic of martial arts. Each school of martial arts sets forth very definite and strict requirements for the postures and movements of every part of the body—hands, eyes, posture, footwork, and so on. Not only must they conform to the technical requirements of martial arts, but at the same time they must also accord with medical science and the principles of energetics. They must also express the esthetics of folk art, as noted earlier.

Once you can fully activate the latent capacities of mind and body, and can modulate capacity at a high level, then this is the highest ideal of movement. In proceeding toward this ideal, martial arts have obtained extremely lofty results, such as are known to few. Modulation of capacity is a core effect produced by the technology of martial arts; it is also the basic principle of health maintenance, and thus constitutes a special feature of martial arts. "Using will rather than force," dynamic thought, higher apperception, union of Nature and humanity, and so on, are all able to efficiently eliminate the tension of physical and mental instincts, the tension of initiative, the tension produced by contradictions between the manifest consciousness and the subconscious, and the tension brought on by all external stimulus (including attacks by adversaries).

In other words, these techniques can eliminate all excessive and inefficient tension, and thus can moderate the biological capacities of the human body and mind to a high degree, and thus enhance the efficiency of biological capacities, at the same time slowing down the process of metabolism and aging in a rational way. Added to the rich training and lofty doctrine of martial arts, this enables people to fulfill an endless quest and find unlimited satisfaction; this enables people to attain spiritual transcendence, and to participate in meaningful human interactions, while always maintaining a relaxed and pleasant state of body and mind. And a healthy body and soul, a positively effective and meaningful life, high efficiency and modulation of capacity, and an appreciation of the beauty of a joyful heart, are the basic secrets of health, well-being, and long life, commonly recognized by people throughout the world.

Anything that causes injury is a most serious matter in exercises involving combat or fighting. Relatively minor injuries cause short-term physical and mental affliction, while serious injuries cause lifetime physical and mental problems. This should be regarded as an obvious truth. Because martial arts are far, far above any sense of winning or losing by fighting, and are furthermore permeated with the principles of medical science, in their essence they present a thoroughly humanistic training and a mode of comparing excellence. If you practice the individual basic exercises and routines of a complete system of training over and over again, at each level there is a higher corresponding medical principle and energetics basis. Pushing-hands and other paired training exercises make a special study of such traditions as checking adversaries out even to the point where their level of attainment can be distinguished from a single gesture or attitude, thus avoiding injury. This can assure that martial artists will continue to heighten their self-defense techniques, while at the same time continuing to make progress in health maintenance and on the path of the search for the Tao.

It is only such a humanistic tradition that enables people past the age of fifty not only to go on practicing endlessly, but also to gain a basis for ceaseless progress throughout the latter half of life toward attainment of total physical and mental sublimation. The highest principles of skilled technique and health maintenance, the highest quest and peak experience, are all preserved within this sort of humanistic training and formalized "competition." Even if people have not set their aims so high, and just practice martial arts for fighting matches, this sort of formalized mode can still greatly reduce damage to body and mind, and lower the rate of injury to the maximum possible degree. To penetrate and to actualize this sort of humanism in the course of pugilistic training and competition is also one of the major features of the noble tradition of martial arts. The highly perfected martial arts by which experts seek to "overcome others' forces without fighting," and by which experts facing each other cannot even make a move, are classic examples of the indivisibility of technical and theoretical principles.

Traditional Chinese culture includes a broad spectrum of religious coloring, within which martial arts are found, showing through with differing degrees of intensity. Classical Chinese philosophy, which is based on Taoism, Buddhism, and Confucianism, already shed their religious components to the maximum possible degree during its formative era; but later it was used by religion to bolster certain theories. Ancient Chinese health arts, including martial arts, were also absorbed and given religious interpretations and applications; and each had its harmful and beneficial influences and effects in religious practices. When science confronted martial arts, it confronted associated biases and superstitions, folly and ignorance; it also confronted some positive results. Fortunately, there are in martial arts themselves standards to test the genuineness of physical and mental praxis; and Chinese religion basically values humanity, not spirits.

As a distinguished English scholar wrote in a book on Taoism, according to Professor Feng Youlan, "Taoism is the world's only mystical system that is not really contradictory to science." This is also evident in the Taoist emphasis on one's fate being in one's own hands, not in the hands of Heaven. This is the positive spirit of struggle to take over the workings of Heaven by mastering Nature through conformity to it. To eliminate the false and keep the true in all phenomena is the perennial task of science; the way it deals with religion is no exception.

To sum up the foregoing remarks, martial arts are a psychophysical format for the essence of the total traditional culture of China, using the science of attack and defense as a basis; they are also Chinese folk forms of physical and mental training and cultivation. Their living spirit is the holistic philosophy of the universe and all things in a hologrammatic interrelationship; their essential message is to seek truth, to seek ideal human character, physique, and spirit; to seek beauty; and to seek kinetic balance and harmonious development of humanity, nature, and society. The tools of martial arts are Eastern epistemology and methodology; their bases are technical breakthrough and rapid advance. These breakthroughs and rapid advances come from the nurturance of the total traditional culture; they require attunement with self-defense, medical science, longevity, universal beauty, ethics, and so on. The most core indication of their standards are the results of refinement of consciousness. Their manifestations are unique physical exercises modeling form and spirit, activation of latent capacities of body and mind, creation of a supranormal constitution, the spectrum of effects realized as results of a combination of elevated efficiency and a high degree of modulation of capacity, and sublimation of the human character and spirit. Their modes of training and ways of assessing victory and defeat all take pacifistic, humanistic forms, and avoid causing injury as much as possible. They can fill people's leisure life with interest and satisfaction, a sense of beauty and enjoyment, thence to attain the goal of extending the life span.

The whole range of past fruits of martial arts provides a boundlessly vast domain of action for modern science, for the present and future of humanity. Martial arts have a meaning and function in future life sciences that cannot be overlooked; they are quietly occupying a unique and irreplaceable position. The aforementioned characteristics of martial arts collectively constitute the value of martial arts, as well as the exceptional features that distinguish martial arts from other systems of physical or mental exercises found throughout the world.

It is precisely because of this, furthermore, that martial arts have not only attracted sports and pugilistics enthusiasts, martial arts have attracted all those who seek to benefit humanity, including scientists, thinkers, artists, literati, scholars, intellectuals, and conscientious people from all walks of life who seek perfect goodness and beauty. It is not very logical at all to limit the value and meaning of martial arts to the domain of physical exercise, because martial arts belong to the domain of the total culture.

As for the relationship of Chinese martial arts with science, there is a serious issue of how studies that have already been relegated to two different logical systems can be reunited. We think that to succeed in this unification it will be necessary to develop methodology and scholarship in which past and present, native and foreign, are combined, with the four quarters complementing and interpenetrating each other. Each party must refine its own strengths, overcome its biases and limitations, go through a process of individual attunement to merge into one whole, and thus form new, altogether more profound, simpler, and more effective ways of thinking and methods of cognizing and transforming the world. Only with a new philosophical and scientific methodology will it be possible to better digest the past and present fruits of world education, science, and culture, and, on the basis of perpetuation of the intellectual essence and crystallization of wisdom of all humanity, to actualize a total breakthrough in human civilization and evolution, a leap of progress in the relationship between humankind and nature, and a sublimation of the vital spirit and mental world of the human race.

All of the results of advanced research into the legacy of history make it clear that humankind is facing a transition of unprecedented magnitude. As in part of the martial arts world, in the whole world of thought and science there is a desire to break through sectarian views in face of this transition, and the new choices it holds for the fate of humanity. The actualization of the decision to collect the total wisdom and knowledge of the past, to disinter latent powers of new wisdom and knowledge, and thus to head for the light, has already presented a most urgent task. The whole tide of political and economic reform in the world today, the trend to coordinate the political and economic relationships among the peoples of all nations, unprecedented developments in communications, ever-increasing cultural and informational exchange—all of these factors will be useful in the creation of a new transition, and will pave the way to an ideal world.

When past and present, native and foreign, are combined together so that they intermingle and assimilate influences from each other, this means that the statuses of the four quarters are all to be equalized in terms of values, government, economics, and dignity, so that they can be objects and tools of research for one another, and can all enjoy the fruits of each other's researches. It is also necessary to establish a similar relationship of dialogue on equal terms between traditional culture and modern science, and between martial arts and modern science. These are all modes of learning that investigate the world and the universe for the benefit of humankind; one should not consider all learning but one's own to be beyond the pale of correct thinking, or stigmatize other learning as antiscientific and superstitious just because of differences in approach, methodology, conceptual framework, and technical vocabulary. We should not forget that the best aspects and purest essence of traditional Chinese culture have developed in the midst of a long and tortuous struggle with prejudice and superstition.

The foregoing descriptions of special characteristics and definitions of methodology are undoubtedly imperfect and rather superficial, but the present volume is not intended to give a full exposition of these ideas. Indeed, the countless mysteries as yet undiscovered and unrecognized by science need cooperative effort and long-term research on the part of all humankind. The purpose of setting forth a simple account of part of the special characteristics of martial arts lies in changing the excessively narrow view of the value of martial arts held by some people. The emphasis on setting forth the issue of a new methodology is a result of personal experience and observation of the many contradictions, difficulties, and obstacles faced by the world of the sciences of the human body.

Some people say there is nothing so special about martial arts, that they are nothing but charlatans' tricks in disguise. Then again, there are also people who make martial arts out to be something altogether mystical and superhuman. The source of both of these biased views is failure to obtain the necessary scientific cross-reference. One of the aims of this book is to seek some degree of resolution to this problem. How this works out, of course, still depends on the evaluation of readers.

The authors are confident that their basic perception of the issues, and their motives and aims, are in accord with the direction of development of martial arts science: martial arts need to head for the future, martial arts need to internationalize. In that process, cultural analysis of martial arts, making martial arts scientific and socially integrated, are some necessary conditions. In order to create these conditions, there is an indispensable precondition; namely, that martial arts be combined with science. This means that martial artists need to grasp modern science, while scientists need to grasp the special character and traditional theories of martial arts. Only thus can both parties find a truly common language, gain a common experience of contradictions, and in the process of cooperating to overcome these contradictions, develop a new scientific methodology for martial arts. The readers of this book may enter into a dialogue with the authors on the profound cultural and social contents of martial arts, the incomparable value of martial arts, and the deep meaning of heading for the world at large and the future to come.

This book does not deal too much with concrete pugilistic principles or exercise methods; it is an inquiry into certain essential characteristics of martial arts, while at the same time being a search for the inner relationship between science and traditional theories, as well as the natural laws governing them. The authors have made a searching inquiry into part of the traditional experiences and concepts of presently existing martial arts, such as the theories of philosophy, culture, and deliberate thought. The authors have no intention of drawing conclusions to the issues under consideration; they are more interested in stimulating readers' thoughts and reactions.

MIND
OVER
MATTER

CHAPTER 1

Refinement of Consciousness through Martial Arts

From refinement of consciousness to dynamic thought to advanced apperception

MARTIAL ARTS EMPHASIZE both mental and physical refinement; all of them emphasize cultivation of the body and cultivation of the mind. The contents of these two major kinds of training must be intimately conjoined and simultaneously fostered, in order to finally attain a high level of cooperation and coordination between the operations of body and mind. These two are inseparable; refinement of the body is inseparable from refinement of the mind, and refinement of the mind is inseparable from refinement of the body.

"Refinement of mind," "refinement of spirit," "cultivation of essential nature," and "refinement of consciousness" are all defined by modern people as different levels and facets of the interrelationships within the domain of the vital spirit and depth psychology. "Refinement of the body," "refinement of the physique," "refinement of vitality," and "refinement of energy" all belong to different levels and facets of what modern people define as the interrelationships within the domain of the material components of the human body. Since refinement of the body and refinement of the mind are both inseparable from refinement of consciousness, here we temporarily use "refinement of consciousness" as an inclusive term.

There have been many successful scientific experiments dealing with cultivation of the body, but most of them have been limited to physical exercise guided by ordinary psychology. When it comes to refinement of consciousness through martial arts, and the conditions of operation of the human body as guided thereby, there have been very few scientific results. The contents of most of these, furthermore, still await further theoretical and technological development, the creation of the necessary conditions, before they will be able to reach such results and interpretations of scientific research as will satisfy modern people. In order to find a solid resting place, moreover, they await the mutual interpenetration and comprehensive study of modern science, ancient Chinese philosophy, Chinese medicine, energetics (*qigong*) and martial arts.

The reader may ask, since there is little basis for scientific research, then how can there be any "scientific refinement of consciousness" to discuss? To this we may give the affirmative answer that without discussion, there is no way to sum up currently existent experience, and no way to create the necessary premises for modern scientific research.

Our reason is quite sufficient: for modern science, and the people of modern times, "refinement of consciousness" in martial arts is virgin ground, very fertile but as yet inaccessible to development. Nevertheless, within the domain of individual physiology, it is already a richly productive source of enormous fruits, strung together like pearls.

The position of refinement of consciousness in the theory and practice of martial arts is utterly critical. It pervades the fundamentals of training in martial arts as well as the most advanced contents of their highest level. This is the technical and theoretical core and quintessence of martial arts. To abandon this is tantamount to throwing away the living soul and fundamental work of the techniques and theories of martial arts, leaving only low level "external exercises" with their peculiarities of outward form, only retaining contents substantially much the same as any other pugilistic techniques.

The inner exercises and energy exercises of martial arts are inseparable from corresponding "consciousness exercises." Without going through the process of refinement of consciousness, there is no way for the inner and outer exercises of martial arts to progress into

04/18/2018

Items checked out to:

   FULLERTON, ALEXANDER R

#100

Mind over matter : higher martial

Barcode   31397001595209

Louisville Adult Nonfiction

Due   05-02-18

Total items checked out 1

**You just saved $24 by using
Rodman Public Library today.**

Thank you for visiting!

Rodman Public Library
330-821-2665
Renew online
www.rodmanlibrary.com

higher levels of effective work and spiritual states. This is the sort of experience alluded to in the folk saying, "If you practice martial arts without practicing meditation, when you get to be old, it will all be in vain."

Thus the refinement of consciousness in martial arts is not only indispensable, it must be considered the core issue of research in martial arts. It needs to be pursued diligently, penetrated deeply, and investigated searchingly. It must be made the subject of special research, and approached in a systematic manner.

Only by bringing out the basic nature of martial arts is it possible to perpetuate them and bring out their essence. Only then can they be modernized and popularized in society at large. And only thus will it be possible to offer Chinese martial arts in a true sense to humankind. And only then can there be a bright future for martial arts. We can even predict that refinement of consciousness will provide the most sophisticated medium for interdisciplinary approaches to countless fields of scientific inquiry.

There are several conditions that are to our advantage. For one thing, we have continuously progressing scientific techniques. For another, in the persons of certain martial artists and masters of energetics who have attained proficiency and accomplished refinement of consciousness, the existence and function of this special consciousness are experiential realities, which have been verified as sensible and perceptible actualities, with differing degrees of understanding and realization.

What is even more valuable, in the many traditional scientific works to be found within classical encyclopedic treatises, classical philosophical texts, and Chinese medical literature, in the theories of traditional martial arts at their highest levels, and in the theories of energetics, there are already a great many relevant writings to which we may refer for insight into the subject.

Our task, in face of this special cultural and scientific heritage, is to work out a new methodology, taking a creative attitude combining the ancient and the modern, the indigenous and the foreign, so as to realize breakthroughs in theory and scientific research.

When it comes to dealing with the modern scientific and intellectual communities, our task lies first of all in producing some sort of representational systematization and ordering of traditional theories and practical results, while at the same time relating this to modern science and its technical terminology, insofar as it is possible, to produce an interpretation or "translation," so to speak.

In the eyes of modern people, this effort may seem prescientific, sub-scientific, or hypothetical in nature; it may seem that the principles and special effects of energetics may be hard to understand and absorb. At the same time, it is hard to avoid producing disparities and discrepancies in the process of interpretation and "translation."

Nevertheless, even though this may be an "adventure" not faced by people of the past in their work, we cannot halt progress unreasonably, and we cannot abandon this task of such great meaning for the whole of humanity.

There are many schools of advanced martial arts, but Chinese martial arts, with all their complex styles and routines, ultimately approach the same goal by different routes. The highest state attained by the various schools of Chinese martial arts is one and the same goal; in this sense, the martial arts may be spoken of as one school. When we discuss advanced martial arts, particularly refinement of consciousness, we find that when we use common terms of one particular subschool, even if they are somewhat different from the terminology of other subschools in their manner of expression, nevertheless the content is often the same.

For this reason, a searching discussion of refinement of consciousness will also yield another important gain, which is to overcome the various sectarian biases that have taken form over the course of history, thus effectively avoiding sectarian disputes. Sectarianism is a tremendous obstacle to the perpetuation and expression of the essence of martial arts, and a hindrance to the emergence of martial arts into the world at large. All serious martial artists know that Chinese martial arts, from their sources and foundations to their highest levels, are originally one school. At the same time, we firmly believe that only today, when ancient and modern science and philosophy are communing and uniting, is it possible to break through these artificial sectarian divisions and bring to light a universal wave of energy.

CHAPTER 2

Martial Arts and Traditional Theories

THE TRADITIONAL THEORIES of which we speak are the traditional Chinese sciences—apart from various ignorant fetishes and superstitions—that are related to refinement of consciousness. In this section, we will present a brief summary of relevant issues and historical materials. In order to avoid bias, for the time being we will not categorize them simplistically into idealism and materialism.

We hope that the reader will be able to keep one idea in mind: just because the conceptual systems and terminologies are not the same as those of modern science, that does not mean we can consider traditional Chinese sciences to be "unscientific." Theory plus practical results and actual effects, naturally forming systematic doctrine, can in principle be recognized as science. We certainly cannot reject rational and effective ancient Eastern modes of thought as being outside the domain of correct thinking just because of differences in premise, angle of approach, system, and concept.

Refinement of Consciousness as the Core of Advanced Training in Martial Arts

A proverb says, "Inwardly cultivating energy, outwardly cultivate sinew, bone, and muscle." This is a common, if crude and shallow, summary of the two main bases of martial arts; cultivation of the body, and cultivation of energy.

This saying makes it clear that cultivation of the body and cultivation of energy are the two core elements of training in martial arts.

In concrete terms, of course, the degree, order, and method of training vary according to the particular pugilistic tradition.

Needless to say, these two kinds of training are inseparable from the human brain, inseparable from corresponding disposition and guidance of consciousness. Guidance of consciousness is indispensable for any exercise and training of the human body, so it is a factor common to all such systems. The distinction between martial arts and other systems of physical training lies in the directing consciousness itself, which must undergo special training. This is the surface meaning of "refinement of consciousness." (The inner meaning of refinement of consciousness will gradually unfold in the course of our discussion.)

The training of consciousness itself includes guidance in ancient Chinese philosophy, Chinese medicine, and the theories of energetics and martial arts. At the same time, it is based on the dynamics of movement of living things, the psychology of exercise, energetics, technique and theory, and the arts of nurturing the body and preserving health. On examination, this training of consciousness permeates the whole body of martial arts, including every level, every facet, and every part.

Because of this, in the simultaneity of cultivation of the body and cultivation of energy, "refinement of consciousness" is a higher level core element within martial arts training. It is also an outstanding basic characteristic of martial arts.

Refinement of Consciousness: Training the Directorate of the Human Body to Activate Supranormal Body-Mind Development

Through training the elements of the "directorate" or "high command" of the human body, there is a concomitant operation of supranormal physical and mental training.

The theory of *Taijiquan* is written in terms such as the following. "Consciousness and energy are the rulers, bones and muscles are the administrators." "Mind is the command, energy is the signal banner." "Operate energy by mind, operate the body by energy; then you can conveniently follow the mind."

From a literary point of view, we can see theories of martial arts draw material for the surface content of their metaphors from the terminologies of feudal class relations, ancient military command systems, and the energetics content in martial arts.

In terms of meaning, consciousness (mind), energy, and the body are clearly defined as three facets or cooperating functions within one indivisible system. Among these, mind is the initiator of systematic movement, so it is the directorate, or high command. Energy is the capacity of systematic movement. The body is the army.

The mind can also be likened to the main switch (or switchboard, or control room), with energy being like the current of electricity. The body is like the wiring and the electronic equipment running on the electricity. The aim of the operation of the system itself requires you to "conveniently follow the mind" in the sense that it is necessary to accord with the intention and will of the directorate, or high command.

From the point of view of systematics, these distinctions in classes of function and order of levels correspond to the interrelation between mind and body, and the principle of simultaneous cultivation of mind and body existing within each school of martial arts and each type of pugilistic technique. It is just that each school has differences in mode of expression and concrete practical procedures. These distinctions in class of function and order of level also correspond to the basic theories of modern science about the relationship between body and mind.

However, while emphasizing the relationship between consciousness and energy as that between ruler and administrator, or as that between command and signal, Chinese martial arts also involve a particular study of correspondences between mind and conscious intent, between consciousness and energy, and between energy and power, as well as the correspondences of the hands and feet, elbows and knees, shoulders and thighs. Martial arts also involve a particular study of mutual correspondence between the internal and the external. Thus martial arts are very particular about the correspondences of total systems. Correspondence means harmony and coordination. But what do these terms imply?

The problem lies in this: within a system reacting to so many illogical (and even unnatural) temporal conditions, the operations of consciousness, energy, and the body have not been able to attain development of genuine cooperation. Accordingly, this has led to the unreasonable auto-dissipation of the vital power of the human body and mind. This leads to wastage of vital power, which in extreme cases can lead to physical and mental illness.

For this reason, humankind needs to think up as many ways as possible of eliminating this sort of waste, and of actualizing the cooperation and coordination of the operations of consciousness, energy, and the body. In the search for realization of this goal, martial arts have obtained very lofty results.

The special characteristic of the course of training in martial arts is as follows. First, basic training of consciousness, energy, and mind is pursued with the guidance of ordinary consciousness. Then another task is presented on this basis, that of refinement of consciousness, which is the core element of martial arts on the higher level. This means transforming the nature of the "high command" or consciousness itself by training, thereby to create the supranormal consciousness peculiar to martial arts.

Now, "consciousness" refers to this supranormal consciousness, which is then used to guide the enhancement of the constitution of the body and energy, causing them to attain a corresponding supranormal level. Going even further to use the supranormal mind and body, through combined refinement of mind and body one reaches the goal of high-level cooperation and coordination of the operations of consciousness, energy, and the body, at each level of the system of their total organization.

From this description, it is evident that the meaning of refinement of consciousness in martial arts is very different in concept from the training of consciousness in modern athletics. The simultaneous refinement and simultaneous use of mind and body, or we might call it the mutual refinement and mutual employment of mind and body, is still not the highest level of refinement of consciousness. There is a higher level, called "using consciousness, not strength," and at another level, yet more advanced, even consciousness is no longer used. Thus it is necessary to "eliminate conscious intent" in order to enter into the exercise of a system of total awareness of supranormal consciousness and physical being.

This latter is the highest level of exercise in coordination, of which it is said, "the nonintentional is supreme," and "consciousness without conscious intent is true consciousness." Only then can one enter into the highest realm of experience.

Refinement of Consciousness and the Triad of Vitality, Energy, and Spirit in Chinese Medicine

In Chinese medical theory relating to the triad of vitality, energy, and spirit, we can see the same sort of division of levels and functional relationships as in the triad of consciousness, energy, and the body in martial arts. Vitality, energy, and spirit each has a number of differences in level and mass, but we will not consider that here for the moment.

Vitality refers to all basic matter constituting the human body and supporting life activities. Here it may be regarded as representative of the "body," which is the "mechanical system."

Energy can be summed up as the "power system" of the human body (including the brain).

Spirit is the total expression of the life activity of vitality and energy, including all spiritual and psychological activity in human beings. Here it may be regarded as representative of "consciousness," which is the "motivation and direction system."

According to the theory of primal energy, the universe and all beings are pervaded by primal energy. All beings contain vitality, energy, and spirit, these just being different states and forms of activity of the primal energy. In this section we have already distinguished among several different kinds of vitality, energy, and spirit.

Vitality, energy, and spirit are three things that function interactively to maintain life in the organic systems of the human body. Vitality and energy constitute the foundation of the spirit, which is the governing director of vitality and energy. Spirit is the normal condition of life activity, and it is also its highest expression.

Here it must be explained that the modern Chinese term "vital spirit" now refers only to the psychological activity of human consciousness, but its original meaning undoubtedly came from Chinese medical theories about vitality, energy, and spirit. Vitality is life (the body), spirit is essence (the mind), energy is a capacity employed by both body and mind. In its original meaning, the term "vital spirit" indicates the total combined biological and psychological efficacy of the human body and mind.

From this we can see how seriously Chinese medicine views the recognition and reason of the inseparability of physical and mental function, and how great a significance it attributes to them. The practical methods associated with this recognition and this reasoning are those we introduce and apply in each chapter of this book. Without these pragmatic methods, there is no way to perceive what consciousness is; it cannot even be described.

In the chapter on the Original Spirit in the classic *The Spiritual Mechanism*, there is a detailed discussion of vitality, spirit, will, thinking processes, and so on. This can be viewed as a general statement of the theory of cognition developed in the psychology of Chinese medicine: "The coming of life is called vitality. Two vitalities maintaining each other is called spirit. What comes and goes with spirit is called the celestial soul. What goes out and in with vitality is called the earthly soul. The means of disposal of affairs is called mind. When the mind has content, that is called consciousness. When consciousness dwells on something, that is called intent. Changes in attention based on intent are called thought. Reaching afar by thought is called consideration. Managing things with consideration is called intelligence."

It is not difficult to see that this passage is at the same time also an early discourse of Chinese medical science relating to the conscious contents of spirit, logic, thought, and science, as well as the relationship between body and mind.

Of course, these terms of Chinese medical science were not established for the purposes of martial arts. The role of Chinese medical science is to fight disease; its fundamental methodology involves using its theories and techniques to combine the sciences of the universe, nature, and life, to regulate the balance of yin and yang in the human body, and thus reach the goal of curing disease.

At the same time, however, Chinese medical science has provided medical and hygienic safeguards for training consciousness, energy, and the body through martial arts. Each branch of martial arts requires a combination of the theory of imaging internal organs, the theory of energy channels, the principle of shifting energy flow at specific times (the "biological clock" of Chinese medicine), and doctrines such as the five shifts and six energies, conjoining the necessary training in Chinese medical science to the progressive development of vitality, energy, and spirit, enabling the human body and mind, both externally and internally to attain the most effective attunement and motor balance.

Coming concretely to refinement of consciousness, Chinese medical science places emphasis on the idea of tuning the psychic mechanism, as illustrated in such sayings as "Curing the spirit is first," or "What is most important is curing the spirit," and "The highest preserve the spirit, the crude preserve the physical body."

There is an even more specialized sense to this. That is, "refinement of consciousness" means cultivation of every level of the "spirit," including all the categories of Chinese medical science relative to the body and mind, especially to the psychological aspect: vitality, spirit, higher and lower souls, mind, attention, will, thought, reflection, and knowledge. It also includes other aspects of the whole spirit, including aspiration, temperament, character, and so on.

The purpose of combining martial arts principles with Chinese medical science is based on linking medical principles, including natural rules of mental and physical hygiene, with the development of human character, spirit, and health, in order to solve the issues involved in cultivating extra-ordinary consciousness, especially the responsibility involved in having a supranormal body and mind; to see to it that these are not used simply for martial arts per se, but also have the pragmatic effect of helping one arrive at improved physical and mental health, preventing sickness and prolonging life.

Refinement of Consciousness and Energetics

Historically speaking, energetics (*qigong*) has been a bridge linking martial arts with Chinese medicine and philosophy. The inner work of martial arts refers, first of all, to energetics. On a more advanced level, it refers to the consciousness exercises corresponding to martial arts assimilated to energetics.

Historically, it was only after martial arts had been combined with conscious energy exercises did they lead to dramatically new effects on human physiology, on the musculature, on the entire psychic system, on dexterity and coordination, and on hygiene and health. Only with the existence of energetics combining pugilistics with hygiene do martial arts come to have the role of refinement of consciousness far beyond the domain of the ordinary psychology and physiology of exercise, as well as the extremely special, even astounding supranormal results thereby produced in the course of physical and mental training in martial arts.

On the other hand, only with martial arts does energetics work lead to a completely new breakthrough and advancement in terms of the level of harmonization of movement and stillness. In other words, each is enriched by the combination of both.

The reason some people have previously declared that martial arts must be combined with energetics is that they saw so many contemporary practitioners of martial arts exercise who did not investigate energetics training. The fact is that martial arts and energetics had already been combined earlier on in history.

Martial arts have become one type of special format and process of energetics training. The reason for renewing emphasis on "combination" is that for several decades martial arts exercises over a wide area have parted ways with energetics, and lost the element of inner work. This is why it is necessary to call for a "revival" of inner work in martial arts, a "revival" of energetics within martial arts. Strictly speaking, martial arts without the inner work of energetics are no longer classical Chinese martial arts, or at least not high level martial arts. To renew the call for "combination of martial arts with energetics" now is no different from calling for combination of martial arts with martial arts.

Similarly energetics work is inseparable from consciousness exercises, because all varieties of energetics require adjustment and training of consciousness.

Schools of energetics belong, in the first place, to corresponding schools of philosophy and medical science. Those among them that have been combined with many schools of martial arts and varieties of pugilism have all formulated a similarly large number of principles and methods of energetics, along with the corresponding consciousness exercises.

Furthermore, all of them have unique exercises and secret teachings, all of them have peak experiences; yet in the highest realms, there is also a tendency for the different paths to ultimately reach the same goal. The main essentials of energetics come from Chinese medical science and the three philosophies of Confucianism, Buddhism, and Taoism, as well as their religious systems, each of which has also produced numerous schools and sects.

Spatial limitations do not permit a full treatment of the complexities of energetics systems in this chapter; so we will limit the discussion to the Taoist theory of "twin cultivation of essence and life" as an example.

Twin cultivation of essence and life is the training of human vitality, energy, and spirit, by means of energetics exercises in stillness and movement, or by means of the methods of inner work in martial arts, in which movement and stillness are combined. Vitality and energy constitute "life," spirit is "essence," but when they are refined to the furthest possible degree, ultimately they are a single energy.

The essential aim in this is to overcome the various physical and mental obstructions formed in human beings by acquired conditioning, so as to realize the goal of returning from the temporal to the primal, reverting to reality and restoring wholeness; and through this process, furthermore, to disinter the latent capacities of the human body and brain.

Although the principle particularly emphasizes twin cultivation and simultaneous refinement, yet under the premise of always requiring twin cultivation, whether simultaneous or alternating, there is also a transition from principal focus on life exercise to principle focus on essence exercises. There are also distinctions between schools that focus principally on essence exercises from start to finish, and those that focus principally on life exercises from start to finish.

The four major levels of Taoist energetics are summarized in these terms: "Refining vitality into energy, refining energy into spirit, refining spirit back into openness, refining openness to merge with the Tao." Although the word "consciousness" is not explicitly mentioned here, obviously all training of vitality, energy, and spirit is inseparable from consciousness, whether one is cultivating life or cultivating essence.

And here the function and purpose of refining consciousness have also been raised a major step higher, this being to elevate the supranormal training of the human mind and body (vitality, energy, and spirit) to reach the same state as that indicated by the highest philosophical principle of Taoism, which is to harmonize with the natural laws of the universe.

This state, furthermore, is the common goal of the different schools of Confucian, Buddhist, and Taoist energetics, because in principle "The Infinite," "The Void," and "The Tao" are different names for the same state. As we can see from this, energetics most certainly form a bridge from martial arts to philosophy, and a channel through which philosophy penetrates martial arts.

The character for the word "essence," referring to the basic nature or essence of humanity, is derived from a combination of elements meaning "mind" and "life," so it may be vulgarly interpreted to mean "the life of the mind," or "the mind that goes on living." This refers to the purest substance or highest expression of the human spirit and human psychology.

Viewed from the angle of refinement of consciousness, the arrangement of the steps in training the attention, energy, and body by means of the method of twin cultivation of essence and life are as follows. Based on the premise of comprehensive refinement and parallel enhancement of the energies of all the internal organs, priorities are established. One starts from refinement of the protective energy (the lower or earthly soul), progresses to refinement of the vital energy (intent, or will), on to refinement of the creative energy (the higher or celestial soul), then again to refinement of the basic energy and basic spirit (emptiness).

All of these stages are inseparable from exercises of consciousness corresponding to each level. Finally one merges with the Tao, which enables a human being to attain a thoroughly fulfilling holistic harmony and coordination with the universe and with Nature, and also to fully employ the results of this training to attain the goals of disinterring extra-ordinary latent capacities and extending the life span.

Commonly known examples of the combinations of Taoist energetics and martial arts include *Taijiquan,* or "Absolute Boxing," *Xingyiquan,* or "Boxing Lending Form to Consciousness," and *Baguaquan,* or "Eight Trigram Boxing." The present work just uses *Taijiquan* as an example.

Guided by the philosophy of the Absolute (*Taiji*), *Taijiquan* lays exceptional emphasis on "parallel refinement of mind and body, twin cultivation of essence and life." Based on these premises, *Taijiquan* also involves a transition, through refinement of consciousness, from primary focus on refinement of the body (refinement of vitality and refinement of energy) to primary focus on refinement of mind (refinement of spirit, cultivation of essence).

Within this process, there is a step-by-step progression from "consciously refining consciousness" through "between consciousness and unconsciousness," to the realm of so-called "no consciousness" in which "consciousness (mind) dies, while the spirit lives." Then, passing through the steps of refining the spirit and refining openness, one realizes the goal of "stability of spirit, plenitude of energy, fulfillment of essential nature, and a constructive life," and then finally returns to the Endless (which is the same as "merging with the Tao").

The rubrics used by the various schools and lineages are not the same, the order of their procedures differs, they are more and less complex or simple, their technical principles and methods each have their own peculiar attainments, and there are differences in the range of their contact with literature, performing arts, and fine arts, as well as distinctions in their levels of depth. In any case, however, refinement of consciousness must go through this kind of orderly progression of ascending levels. Furthermore, the higher they go, the more they show the tendency of these different paths to lead ultimately to the same goal. All the schools recognize this.

This sort of training, characterized by progressive ascent through successive levels, not only helps the human body-mind system to attain harmony and coordination in movement, as well as open up endless vistas of development of the latent capacities of the human body and brain. It also enables people to realize the highest level of dynamic balance, harmonization, and unification within their own body-mind, as well as with the outside world, including both Nature and society.

There is something that must also be noted in order to fill out this picture. Speaking in general terms, medical energetics work places most emphasis on maintaining health, Confucian energetics work places most emphasis on moral virtue, while Buddhist energetics work and Taoist energetics work have similarities and differences. Leaving aside the highly developed people of both schools who transmitted extraordinary forms, speaking in terms of the total effect of actual practice, the results of the life-exercises of Taoism are higher than those of its essence-exercises, whereas the results of the essence-exercises of Buddhism are higher than those of its life-exercises. Because of this, differences exist in the levels of refinement of consciousness. (To delve deeply into the inner secrets of the essence-exercises of Buddhism and dig them out is a task that is not to be slighted.)

The theory of advanced Chinese energetics repeatedly emphasizes the union of the four schools of Confucianism, Buddhism, Taoism, and medical science. Chinese energetics work is a single science requiring a high level of integration and interpenetration of the practical principles and actual results of the four schools. However, in the process of actual training, the differences among the individual schools still appear until the actual attainment of the highest realm.

If we use modern terminology to summarize the distinctions among the four schools, it is hard to avoid creating biased discrimination. Nevertheless, we may still summarize them as follows to let modern people get some sense of them. Buddhism is advanced psychology, Taoism is natural science and bioscience. Confucianism is sociology and social relations, medicine is medical science. For the four schools to attain complete communion and interchange, until they reach integration on a broad scale (and not just among a small number of people) still awaits further efforts.

Refinement of Consciousness and Classical Chinese Philosophy

Martial arts are forms of body-mind exercise evolved from combinations of pugilistic technique, medical science, energetics, philosophy, and other cultural traditions, including literature, performing arts, fine arts, and so on. Pugilism availed itself of medical science and energetics to connect with philosophy, literature, and the arts. Because of this, the activity of refining consciousness found its highest sublimation in philosophy.

This means that we should not restrict the content of martial arts to a systematization of any particular part thereof; it is imperative to have a comprehensive view of the sources. It is precisely because of this that martial arts can reach high levels of human wisdom through the process of martial arts, even to the point where they reach such peak experiences of analogical comprehension that they can comprehend everything at once.

Conversely, the contribution of martial arts to philosophy is also indelible. Martial arts have themselves provided a shining model for the concrete experience of philosophy, and have also provided hard to obtain experimental evidences relevant to a number of central issues of philosophy. At the same time, through the highest attainments of refinement of consciousness, martial arts, along with the peak experiences found in Chinese medicine, energetics, literature, and the arts, transformed the literary background of classical philosophy, as well as underlying non-literary content, so as to have made it possible to transmit living exemplars and formats even up to the present day.

When we study the issue of refinement of consciousness in martial arts, we cannot but delve into classical Chinese philosophy, because the "consciousness" to which we refer is a product of the practical methodology of Chinese philosophy. Because of this, it is necessary to point out emphatically that when we study the precious legacy of classical Chinese philosophy and the products of its various branches, we must be careful not to take up simplifications and vulgarizations which would lead to the sort of attitude with which a dwarf views a giant, or the attitude of blind men feeling an elephant. And we absolutely cannot make this philosophy into a passive object of scientific research, or a dead specimen, without actual experiential evidence.

Because classical Chinese philosophy has its own standpoint, point of view, and methodology, it is a form of thought perpetuated by the Chinese up to the present day; and it uses its own methods to grasp the subjective and objective worlds. In ancient China, before the existence of modern scientific technology and modern thinking methods, the Chinese people were using this sort of method to recognize and reconstruct the subjective and objective worlds, creating a brilliant spiritual and material culture. And in the present day, it has attracted many scientists and philosophers, both Chinese and non-Chinese, with great fascination.

In view of these facts, classical Chinese philosophy has the right to carry on dialogue with modern science and philosophy on an equal footing, in order to better grasp the subjective and objective worlds, and make a new contribution to the welfare of humankind. It is essential to know that among the special capacities realized as results of Chinese medicine, energetics, and martial arts, a number of which have already been authenticated as real facts, there are many—especially certain astounding miracles wrought for the benefit of humanity—that modern philosophy and science have no way to explain. Yet these too are products conceived and developed by Chinese philosophical thought.

While there are still some places in the body of classical Chinese philosophy itself that await organization, purification, development, and elevation, nevertheless its value for the present and future of humankind is incomparable. Chinese philosophy is the brain of the ancient Chinese people, the core of the deep structure of the psychology of the culture, the crystallization of the knowledge and wisdom of the Chinese people.

Summing up ancient Chinese culture, science, arts, social developments, and life experiences, classical philosophy has conversely also become a living spirit and guide for each domain of society and life. Study of martial arts as a whole, including its essence, which is refinement of consciousness, is unquestionably inseparable from philosophy. In this there lies the most urgent matter of "useful application of the ancient in the present."

Classical Chinese philosophy emphasizes a holistic view of Nature, in which Heaven, Earth, and humanity commune, Heaven and humanity sense and respond to each other, Heaven and humanity unite, Heaven, Earth, and humanity join as one, body and mind unify, and so on. Once this type of philosophical principle was born, it immediately formulated the unified body of traditional Chinese science and culture.

Strictly speaking, ancient Chinese science and culture are not separate fields of learning. Even if they investigate different levels and facets of the macroscopic world and the microscopic world, they do not isolate a single level or facet from the whole for research. They always pursue their investigations in the context of the totality, never forgetting the whole. This is a very different methodology from that of Western science and thought, which split up the whole, minutely examine parts isolated from the totality, and then struggle to rediscover a connection with the whole.

Thus what appear to modern people to be completely different fields of learning were one continuity in the minds of the ancient Chinese, a single unified system following a single unified order. Martial arts, energetics, Chinese medicine, philosophy, matter, spirit, physics, chemistry, mathematics, biosciences, and so on—in terms of modern science, these have very different principles and involve dissimilar objects of research. In the view of the ancient Chinese, however, even if these have their own individual peculiarities, nevertheless they are all phenomena that follow one great law and are part of one integral system.

Humankind is none other than a microcosm, a hologram of the total system of the universe, in complete communion with the macrocosm. Body, energy, and consciousness in martial arts correspond to vitality, energy, and spirit in Chinese medicine and energetics; they are in the same vein as Earth, humanity, and Heaven in philosophy, corresponding respectively. Consciousness, body, and energy in martial arts are simply manifestations of the relationships among Heaven, Earth, and humanity within the human body.

According to Chinese philosophy, Heaven and Earth (yin and yang) interact to produce all beings and all things, including humankind. In the human body, consciousness is Heaven, the body is Earth; the energy of the interaction of Heaven (consciousness) and Earth (the body) constitutes the "energy" of the life force in the human body. When the primal energy in human beings is in harmony with the energy produced by the interaction of Heaven and Earth, this constitutes the foundation of human life and health. In the temporal development of human beings, any energy that is not in harmony with the energy of the interaction of Heaven and Earth (i.e. that portion of yin and yang energy that cannot commune and equilibrate within the human body) has in it a source of human illness, physical and mental.

Because of this, no matter what the angle of approach—be it martial arts, energetics, Chinese medicine, psychology, philosophy, Nature, or society—there is only one purpose to the training and education, namely the continuous elevation of the degree of communion and balance of yin and yang energies in the human body, enabling them to attain the maximum harmony and balance with the macrocosmic Heaven and Earth.

Similarly, no matter which of countless angles we view the matter from—pugilism, health, cultivation of conduct and character, human life, philosophical principles, fine arts, culture, science, and so on— the purpose of the exercise and refinement of consciousness in martial arts is all a matter of taking the already unbalanced relationship between body and mind, and putting it through training and tuning to restore the unity of Heaven and humanity, a balance in which subject and object are unified.

To correctly resolve the issue of unification of subject and object, ultimately reaching the state of "merging in union," and accordingly to correctly make use of the principles of unification of Heaven and humanity, is properly the common task of philosophy and martial arts, as well as the other arts and sciences. At the same time, we must repeatedly emphasize that martial arts and Chinese philosophy, as well as any branch of learning in this overall system, fully has the right and the ability to use its own methods to study modern science.

It is precisely this natural order and philosophical principle of the hologrammatic mutual inclusion of the whole and the parts that has brought about the resulting hologrammatic mutual inclusion of martial arts and philosophy, making martial arts inseparable from philosophy, and philosophy (within a certain range) inseparable from martial arts, making martial arts lead to philosophy and philosophy to martial arts. By the same principle, whether it be martial arts or philosophy, both together constitute a domain of research in which many modern fields of study intersect and interrelate.

From the time of the earliest shell and bone inscriptions accessible today, and the special comprehensive work known as the *I Ching,* classical Chinese philosophy has gone through number of phases. There was the founding of Confucianism and Taoism, the contentions of the Hundred Schools of the Warring States era (5th–3rd centuries B.C.E.), the classical scholarship of the Han dynasty (206 B.C.E.–220 C.E.), the mysticism of the Wei and Jin dynasties (220–419), and the Buddhist learning of the Northern and Southern dynasties (420–581) through the Sui (581–618) and Tang (618–906) dynasties. Coming to the Song (960–1278), Yuan (1278–1368), Ming (1368–1644), and Qing (1644–1911) dynasties, Confucian, Buddhist, and Taoist ideas were combined to form the School of Principle characteristic of the Song and Ming dynasties. Finally, the introspective thought of the Ming and Qing dynasties evolved into the modern stage of development of Chinese philosophy.

In the course of this long process of development, many disputes took place between Confucians and Taoists, between Taoists and Buddhists, between Buddhists and Confucians, and so on. The three teachings also mutually influenced, absorbed, and combined with each other over a long period of time. The final round of mutual conflict and mutual interpenetration was the origin and development of the Song and Ming dynasty School of Principle, also called the School of the Way.

In the combination of the three teachings made by the School of Principle, the mainstay is Confucianism, with some of the fruits of Buddhist and Taoist philosophy being adopted into the Confucian system. For Confucianism, this was undoubtedly an unprecedented improvement, but for Buddhism and Taoism it had the effect of fragmentation of the spirit, even to the point of distortion, devaluation, and obscuration.

Even so, three major doctrinal trends emerged within the School of Principle . These three major doctrinal trends manifested the historical controversies of Taoism, Buddhism, and Confucianism within the domain of the School of Principle. Among them, the doctrine of principle as fundamental represents Confucianism, which is based on moral virtues; the doctrine of energy as fundamental represents Taoism, which is based on the Tao (energy); the doctrine of mind as fundamental represents Buddhism, which is based on mind (essence).

However, in this synthesis, the factions based on mind and energy generally strove to prove themselves to be the ones who were in accord with "principle," trying to show that "mind" itself is principle, or that "principle" means the order according to which energy operates. In any case, all of them were Confucians at the core, and were working for the cause of the Confucian School of Principle.

The purpose of relating these historical developments is to point out two facts about martial arts and refinement of consciousness. One is that Taoism, Buddhism, and Confucianism were all exploited for political purposes by the feudal ruling class; in particular, the political exploitation of Confucianism was most serious and long-lasting, mainly from the time of the Confucian scholar Dong Zhong-shu four centuries after the death of Confucius through the Confucians of the Song and Ming dynasties.

The second fact has to do with Chinese medical science, energetics, martial arts, and some of the Taoism and Buddhism that made the greatest contributions in other fields. They were subjected to severe suppression by Song and Ming dynasty Confucianism. This suppression lasted so long, nearly one thousand years, that the after-effects have still not yet disappeared today. This is one of the many reasons for the difficulty we have today in disinterring and setting in order the essences of Buddhist and Taoist philosophy as well as the treasures of Chinese medicine, energetics, and martial arts.

Confucianism belongs more to the system of traditional Chinese political science and social morality; it is as if it were the self-consciousness department in the deep structure of the psychology of the traditional culture of the Chinese people. Buddhist and Taoist philosophy, on the other hand, especially Taoism, which arose and developed in China, tend to reflect more the natural consciousness and subconsciousness in this deep structure, as well as the effort to raise the subconscious to the level of consciousness.

The inner structure of Song and Ming dynasty Neo-Confucianism manifests the constraint, rejection, and suppression of the subconscious and natural consciousness by the self-consciousness (as conditioned by feudal ethics). Even though both Buddhism and Taoism were exploited by the bureaucracy over the generations, nevertheless they formulated natural philosophy and a kind of psychological science; they also represent the subconscious of the people, and have essentially never submitted to the Confucian social consciousness and its repressive policies. *Journey to the West,* the earliest Chinese mythological novel (dating from the 16th century), is a classic example of a famous work of literature reflecting this sort of controversy among Confucianism, Buddhism, and Taoism under the rule of Song and Ming dynasty Neo-Confucianism.

When we study martial arts and their mechanisms for refinement of consciousness, we can by no means avoid the philosophical issues of the highest sublimation and the highest state that can be realized; and we cannot avoid issues connected with ordinary psychology as well as extra-ordinary or supranormal psychology. From modern psychology we know that human consciousness is multitiered, and that this gives rise to an intricate and complex relationship within the biological organism, which is also a multitiered system.

A lack of harmony between the levels of manifest consciousness and the subconscious can make an individual physically and mentally ill. This can cause an individual to unconsciously expend a major proportion of vital energy on this internal contradiction, with the result that there is no vital energy left over for effective use.

Conversely, a rational communion and high degree of harmony between these two levels of consciousness can minimize one's expenditure of physical and mental energy. This can also liberate a maximum amount of vital energy for use in effective living, in study and work. At the same time, it leads people to a dynamic, highly integrated union with the world around them.

This is a kind of release of the latent potential of the human body and brain; and it is also a way toward resolution of a number of social problems. From human societies consisting of millions of individuals, down to a single individual, all alike still await the full opening and development of this sort of latent potential in the broadest possible range. With such a higher purpose, the work of once again disinterring and reordering the legacy of classical Chinese philosophy takes on a completely new significance.

Refinement of consciousness through martial arts, and the results attained thereby, are well able to help us penetrate and comprehend the essence of classical philosophy, perceiving the deep structure of the psychology of Chinese culture from a more advanced level of supranormal consciousness. At the same time, for the purpose of weeding out the false and preserving the true in this enormous legacy, to eliminate the coarse and take the fine, refinement of consciousness through martial arts can serve, from a special domain and a special angle, as a tool and a standard for practical experimentation. In this sense, the function of martial arts is irreplaceable.

This topic is endless, because "consciousness" is something in which body and mind intermingle, the physical and the spiritual intercommunicate, and biology and psychology intersect. It is of a holistic nature, touching upon every domain of human life.

Refinement of consciousness certainly cannot be simply reduced to exercises in active and passive consciousness, just as martial arts cannot be simply reduced to techniques of striking and parrying, offense and defense. Any sort of partial perception can diminish the overall value of martial arts. The five aspects outlined above cannot sum up the total picture of the place of refinement of consciousness through martial arts in the context of traditional theories and practices. They can only be viewed as one spot of a leopard, an indication by which one may take note of the whole.

Martial arts are a total format combining Nature, society, and human life, a system with many levels of effective capacity as well as a holistic essence and potential. The purpose of refinement of consciousness through martial arts is to develop the latent abilities of the human body and brain, to cultivate supranormal capacities in the human body and supranormal powers of consciousness.

Martial arts, particularly in its refinement of consciousness, has a unique epistemology and methodology, a unique theoretical foundation, and a unique system of training and effects on the human body. Measured on the scale of human knowledge, it belongs to a high level of cognition; it is not in the domain of lower levels of cognition. The philosophical foundation of the essence of martial arts, including refinement of consciousness, does not belong to religious superstitions like those recognized by so many modern philosophers, which are anesthetics to enable people to passively avoid the world. To the contrary, the essence of martial arts fully awakens the subjective dynamism of the individual, so that one not only perceives subjective and objective patterns of order; one also masters and employs these subjective and objective patterns of order.

It is not, however, a matter of the inflexible striking the unyielding; it is not a matter of "conquering" nature by destroying nature. It is a matter of employing methods of skillfully "taking over the work of Nature" to master and utilize nature based on the premise of harmonizing with the total order of nature and adapting to it.

CHAPTER 3

What Is Consciousness?

SPEAKING IN BROAD terms, when it comes to the concept of "consciousness" and its implications, traditional Chinese science and culture, literature and arts, medical science, philosophy, energetics, martial arts, and so on, have a kind of conscious perception which has not yet been precisely defined, even to this day. This single point is already a major issue awaiting cooperative research combining numerous subjects. At the same time, each field has its own special perception of consciousness, its own understanding, experience, method of training, and concrete expression of consciousness. The "spirit" or "consciousness" as envisioned in philosophy, Chinese medicine, and Chinese arts; the "consciousness" reached in the realms of ideas in poetry, song, calligraphy, and painting; the "consciousness" and "true consciousness" in the theory of energetics and in martial arts—all these refer to "consciousness," or content related to consciousness.

We may be sure of one thing: that this usage of "consciousness" is a product of a special mode of thought utilized by ancient Chinese in the process of cognizing and transforming the subjective and objective worlds. That is to say, it is a unique product of traditional Chinese culture and psychological structure. Because its angle of approach and method of operation are not the same as those of modern science, therefore its corroboration of phenomena and its course of training are not the same, and so its theory and practical results are also not the same.

Thus we can say that the term "consciousness" covers all levels of consciousness and psychology, containing a crystallization of part of a certain kind of psychological knowledge with special content, form, and meaning. It is also an object of research which the massive psychological systems of the present age have yet to delve into authentically and look into seriously. By its own unique mode of association, it contains a considerable amount of the contents of modern biology and psychology; at the same time, it also touches upon domains of neurological activity, thought, and consciousness at a level of sophistication not as yet even mentioned by modern biological and psychological sciences.

A creative investigative attitude toward the theory and practice of refinement of consciousness through martial arts, drawing on a synthesis of the ancient and the modern, the Chinese and the non-Chinese, can undoubtedly enable us to attain a breakthrough in the question of investigating the fundamental essence of "consciousness," and go on to galvanize breakthroughs in research on subjects in all domains connected with this issue.

Speaking in narrow terms, "consciousness" is a kind of developed mind in which the biological and the psychological are forged together into one. This is represent by the expressions "consciousness and body refined together, exercising both physically and mentally, cultivating essence and life as a pair." We call this "supranormal" consciousness. What is supranormal about it is that this sort of consciousness has gone through combined refinement of consciousness and the body, to reach a level of psychophysical coordination; the supranormal quality is in the ability of this consciousness to to coordinate, activate, and direct biological capacities.

Consciousness as we use it here does not mean consciousness in the ordinary sense, abstract logical thought, or abstract ideation; neither is it formal thinking in the ordinary sense. It is not a building in the brains of a builder, not a form or sound in the brain of a physicist. Nor is it the id, ego, superego, consciousness, subconscious, or instinct as conceived by psychoanalysts. The consciousness of which we speak is in every case developed consciousness; in whatever domain, it is always a result of combined refinement of body and mind.

32

Consciousness is a spiritual-material structure, consisting of a triad of information, capacity, and format. Only when it can perform effectively as such a structure can it function interactively with any spirit or matter at all. Consciousness has a field, and it has force; it is a supranormal consciousness whose own inherent capacity can activate other capacities, forming a potent force field.

Except for a few coincidences, "consciousness" in this sense is not innate. It is a highly ordered consciousness that has gone through special conscious training (and, under some conditions, unconscious training) and has gone through simultaneous refinement of body and mind. This sort of developed consciousness is referred to in martial arts by the expressions "use consciousness, not strength," and "all this is consciousness." In calligraphy and Chinese painting, it is referred to by the expressions "consciousness precedes the brush," and "the effective work is outside the brush."

In the concrete context of martial arts, consciousness means "martial arts consciousness." This kind of consciousness is a comprehensive structure uniting philosophy, psychology, biology, medical science, principles and techniques of self-defense, dynamics, energetics, quintessential ethics, fine arts, and numerous other fields of science and culture.

For the time being, we will make the following definition. "Martial arts consciousness" is a special physical and mental capacity peculiar to the essence of martial arts, attainable only through training in martial arts, which gives rise to a holistic relationship with the mental and biological totality of other human beings as well with the outside world (including Nature and society), enabling the inside and outside of the human body, the spirit and the matter, to interact effectively.

Speaking in terms of this definition, "refinement of consciousness" is training in martial arts consciousness (that is, the special mind-body training of martial arts). In other words, it is the superordinary training of the human body and mind, especially conscious perception, by martial arts.

It should also be explained that not all schools of martial arts or types of pugilism actually refine consciousness. Those that have strength, speed, and endurance at the core of their basic training, those whose purpose is to enhance and strengthen existing reactive power, including their physical techniques and psychological training, do not have the classical characteristics of advanced Chinese martial arts, speaking in terms of dynamics and psychology; even if they do involve a certain amount of conscious psychological training, this sort of training is in any case basically the same in all pugilistic exercise.

Among the non-classical schools of martial arts, there are some kinds of pugilism that have newly combined with energetics, or have made some breakthroughs by certain special exercises, but from the point of view of refinement of consciousness, these can be considered bastardizations.

In advanced types of pugilism, there are also many differences in the degree and level of refinement of consciousness in individual martial artists. People who have clearly and obviously perfected refinement of consciousness are comparatively rare. Even fewer are those who have reached the level of "no conscious intent."

CHAPTER 4

Using Consciousness to Refine Consciousness

Mind: Distinctions between Ancient and Modern Concepts

IN THE FOREGOING section, we noted that "consciousness" refers to a special effective structure in which "spirit and matter are united into one." Here we must present a concept with a more crucial meaning. Without this concept, there is no way to correctly perceive that refinement of consciousness is the essence and true nature of martial arts.

As explained earlier, the fundamental contents of martial arts training are the human vitality, energy, and spirit, which could also be summed up as the mind in which matter, capacity, and spirit are united into one.

The reader may ask how the mind can be this, that, and the other thing. In reality, what modern medical science speaks of in terms of advanced neurological activity also refers to "mind" in which biology, psychology, and capacity are combined into one. This includes material biology and intellectual and emotional activity, as well as the process of growth and change (although it does not include the total human body and mind), which also belong theoretically and pragmatically to different fields of study.

This sort of "belonging" originated as an expedient for purposes of research; used too long, eventually it led to "forgetting the root," with the result that each field of study came to have its own "rules." Even if every single specialized work emphatically points out its subordinate relationship to a totality, nevertheless the habit and conceptual bias of self-contained systems make it extremely difficult for people to find the comprehensive order of the totality and how specialized fields of study ultimately relate to the whole.

The "mind" of which we speak, in which a fundamental triad is united, includes all levels of the total material substance (in the modern sense) of the human body and brain, and it also includes the whole of the human spirit (in the modern sense). Since it includes both the most primitive and the most advanced biology and consciousness, it contains all of the physical and mental capacities latent in human beings. Since it represents both structure and efficacy—the meaning of efficacy being higher than the meaning of structure—at the same time it includes the total capacity by which the human body and mind are able to survive and function. In terms of the concepts of Chinese medicine, all of this can be summed up as vitality, energy, and spirit.

Refinement of mind addresses the various contradictions and obstructions temporally produced within the body and mind, which are inseparable. It involves a training of the totality, using mind to refine the body, using the body to refine the body, using the body to refine the mind, using unminding to refine the mind, and so on. The aim is to eliminate every sort of contradiction inhibiting the cooperative action of body and mind, so as to reach unification of body and mind, oneness of body and mind, and coordination of body and mind.

Herein, both body and mind (or the three facets of mind, which are vitality, energy, and spirit) should be considered necessary parties to unification, the triplex system of capacity, power, and effect that is to be "turned from three into one." The "mind" which is the final product should be considered a single effective system in which the three have already been united into one. This is called the mind that has "returned to reality and gone back to simplicity, mind and energy united, mind and spirit united, mind and consciousness united, spirit and consciousness united," and so on. This alone qualifies as the aim of advanced training in martial arts.

In this mind, there is no division between spirit and matter (this sort of distinction only exists in the conceptions of philosophers). Only with this kind of "mind" do we accord with the fundamental meaning of classical Oriental and Chinese philosophy; only thus do we accord with the highest theoretical and practical objectives sought at the advanced levels of martial arts and energetics; only thus do we accord with the theory of the "real human being" in traditional Chinese medical science. Moreover, having such a "mind" is the goal toward which various schools of martial arts proceed, albeit by different routes. Only with such a mind is it possible to attain a correct holistic relationship with the universe, Nature, and society, so as to achieve harmony and coordination, thus to attain "unity."

This discussion has used the concept of "mind" as an example to explain the greatest, and indeed the most basic, distinction between the system of traditional Chinese scientific concepts and the system of modern scientific concepts. Similarly, it explains the most evident and most central distinction between the concepts employed in martial arts and the concepts employed in the science of exercise in modern physical education.

It is extremely difficult to discuss any issue of advanced martial arts without these clarifications. In particular, there is otherwise no way to talk about issues such as "consciousness," "refining consciousness," "using consciousness to refine consciousness," and "consciousness without conscious intent." Thus in this book it is impossible to avoid using terminology which appears similar on the literal surface but whose conceptual range is divided into two separate meaning systems; we hope the reader will be careful to make these distinctions.

With this in mind, we can go back and talk about orthodox tradition.

The Uncanny Sphere: Where the Whole Body Is Instantly Activated at the Tug of a Single Hair

From whatever angle one views advanced martial arts, they train human vitality, energy, and spirit through various modes of simultaneous refinement of body and mind. The principles and methods of practice are very numerous; we have just pursued a single vein to make a sort of outline analysis by way of introduction. A complete and comprehensive discussion still awaits collective research and effort on the part of the world of martial arts sciences.

The forms of martial arts training do not go beyond the various kinds of standing exercise, deliberate sitting, simplex forms (simple movements), routines, implements, and some other effective auxiliary training. The teaching of the principles of the exercises progresses according to advancement in the level of practical work. Whether it be standing work or moving work, all exercises begin with attunement of the physical form. The attunement of the physical form must be arranged consciously, so it can be said that ultimately we start from attunement of consciousness.

Attunement of the physical form undoubtedly can induce conscious and unconscious changes in the state of the breathing, as well as changes in the state of energy and inner force. The results of this attunement all should bring about a psychological attunement, and then lead to attunement of the consciousness cultivating the exercises. The feedback goes on, as refinement of consciousness fosters the progress of refinement of mind, refinement of energy (including breathing), and refinement of the body (or physical form); and then the tuning of the physical form is again arranged by a new consciousness adapted to new conditions.

At this point, the whole training forms an uncanny sphere, in which each step functions cooperatively with every other step, spiraling upward, going higher stage by stage in an endless ring: consciously tuning the physical form, then consciously and physically inducing and directing psychic force and energy; then using consciousness, physical form, and energy to tune mind; then returning, with consciousness that has been elevated and refined to a higher level by consciously going through training of the physique, energy, and mind, to further train the physique, energy, mind, and "consciousness."

Thus the spiral continues on and on ad infinitum, though never at any point apart from consciousness, the whole cyclical process forming a cycle of deliberate refinement of consciousness. In the course of this cycle, level after level of transformations in vitality, energy, and spirit take place through their mutual refinement and mutual transmutation. For the moment, however, we will simply sum these all up in the terms vitality, energy, and spirit.

Regarding the process of this repeated cyclic training of vitality, energy, and spirit (i.e. of "mind) we can see that consciousness is always a medium and an instrument, yet at the same time it is itself the object of training. Being an instrument, it is also an object of treatment; herein the image and conceptual pattern of using consciousness to refine consciousness is already evident.

To further develop this theme, we can take this kind of special martial arts training of the human body and mind, compare it to a special manufacturing process making a special product, and then analyze "consciousness" and the various principles of how to use consciousness to refine consciousness.

Any manufacturing process includes three elements: raw materials, tools, and tool operators. However, in ordinary manufacturing processes, the people (those who operate the tools), the tools, and the raw materials are three separate entities; whereas in martial arts training, all three are human, all are the human body and mind (or the three facets of the triplex unified "mind").

In ordinary manufacturing, people use tools on raw materials to process or treat them in some way; this is a unilateral, or unidirectional, process. After the product is made, it is an independent entity, from which point on the three elements can be disassociated. In martial arts training, in contrast, everything takes place in the human body; when there is an action, there is a reaction, and the three elements are always interacting, and are all being trained and transformed together in the process of their interaction, causing the totality of the human body and mind to be attuned step by step.

Because of this, whatever change takes place at any point in the course of such training, that will evoke a response from the totality. This is what is referred to by the expression, "tug a single hair, and it moves the whole body."

The Emergence and Function of Consciousness

In martial arts, the most fundamental objects of processing (i.e. the raw materials) are vitality, energy, and spirit. The processing instrument is consciousness. We take the whole exercise system—including the gathering of concentration power, will, motor awareness, symbolic representations of exercise movements, memorization of exercise movements, the key exercise center of the brain, and so on—and temporarily reduce it all to "consciousness," or "conscious intent in movement," which we will for now shorten to "conscious intent," where "the recollection of something in mind is called conscious, the sustaining of consciousness on a particular point is called intent."

The operator of the instrument is also consciousness, to which we relegate ordinary thought, including both logical thinking and thinking in imagery. This thought is defined in terms of intentional modification of mental content, and the mental forms thereof.

Let us first observe the results of the interaction of the raw material, the instrument, and the operator. "Thought" activates "intent" to process vitality, energy, and spirit. The resulting changes in vitality, energy, and spirit are then fed back to produce changes in conscious intent, these two changes are reflected in thought, and this produces certain levels of change in thought.

In the course of their interaction, all three give rise to changes. If the method is correct, these changes are enhancements. They are improvements of their qualitative and quantitative levels, as well as of their capacity for combination and cooperation.

Martial arts training has a key result that is distinct from other forms of exercise. In the course of the interaction of vitality, energy, and spirit with intent, something new is produced. This is the "consciousness" in which vitality, energy, and spirit are united with intent, which is able to cause intent to move in coordination with vitality, energy, and spirit.

This third kind of consciousness, once produced, can simultaneously act on intent as well as on vitality, energy, and spirit; and in the process of absorbing nutrition from these, consciousness is expanded and elevated. "Refinement of consciousness" in martial arts refers primarily to this third kind of consciousness.

Consciousness brings a fourth element to the three aspects of production. Then what is the proper place of each of these four elements in the process of production, and what function does each perform? In these four aspects of the process—Thought," "intent," "consciousness," and "vitality-energy-spirit"—there are three kinds of consciousness.

The first kind is thought, or thinking, which under the continuous influence of the other three will undergo profound changes, leading to a transformation of the method, mode, and content of the individual's thinking. With each level of change in the latter three, which are based on supranormal consciousness, and each level of change in their interaction, there is an inevitable influence on one's way of thought.

The advancement of each level of work, furthermore, is impossible without changes in the way of thinking; otherwise the work does not progress. When the latter three elements have developed to a certain degree, the way of thought will undergo qualitative and quantitative change, enabling people to master the ancient Chinese way of thought by going through the experience of mutual refinement of mind and body. And only with this way of thinking is it possible to open up the portals to the realms of the higher levels of martial arts and energetics for people of the present day.

The second kind of consciousness is intent. Having transformed vitality, energy, and spirit through the instrumentality of intent, and thus having transformed oneself, there is produced a consciousness in which intent has united with vitality, energy, and spirit to form a single organism. After this, intent as an instrument must carry out a process of treatment of two kinds of raw materials: consciousness and vitality-energy-spirit.

The function of intent here is to combine as much as possible of the element of will and the elements of vitality, energy, and spirit, refining them together to produce consciousness. In the course of this process, furthermore, the level, quality, and quantity of "consciousness" are elevated to the point where a certain specific amount of intent and vitality-energy-spirit are thoroughly melded to produce a high level of consciousness having highly enhanced qualitative and quantitative capacities, thereby to attain to a coordination of stillness and movement in consciousness, energy, and spirit.

In this process, intent gradually dissolves and melds; transmuting itself as of a finite capacity, it also reconstructs and enhances its extra capacity; dissolving vitality-energy-spirit as a finite capacity, it reconstructs and enhances the extra capacity of vitality, energy, and spirit. Removing a major part of the barrier between thought and intent, it enables thought and intent to communicate directly, gaining a relationship of direct coordination.

Thought that has gone through the process of reconstitution thereafter acts directly on consciousness without the mediation of intent. Through consciousness, furthermore, it acts indirectly on that part of intent that has been reconstructed but not yet refined into consciousness, as well as on vitality, energy, and spirit.

At the same time, that part of intent that has not yet been refined into consciousness continues to act on consciousness, and on vitality, energy, and spirit, causing all these to interact. This interaction itself also continues to act on thought. Thus is formed the complex process of the mutual refinement of the four elements and the conscious refinement of consciousness.

The System of Conscious Refinement of Consciousness: "Division," "Interruption," and "Combination"

The addition of the third kind of consciousness causes the whole training to manifest a multilevel system of using consciousness to refine consciousness, going through a multitiered process of applying conscious refinement of consciousness to vitality, energy, and spirit, thus producing various kinds of feedback. Thought and consciousness interact, thought and intent interact, intent and consciousness interact; these three levels of using consciousness to refine consciousness so that consciousness refines consciousness (that is, different levels of consciousness refine each other) cause the interaction of the three levels themselves to act upon thought, intent, and consciousness, which action could also be considered part of a fourth level function.

What is more, vitality, energy, and spirit also individually produce three levels of interaction with thought, intent, and consciousness. The interaction of these three levels themselves also then brings about action and response on four fronts. The four levels in consciousness and the four levels of vitality, energy, and spirit then go on to produce an even more complex interaction. This interpenetrating, interwoven training causes the totality of the human body and mind to give rise to a transmutation, from the body and mind of an ordinary person to a supranormal body and mind.

The important point, however, in the deliberate technology of using consciousness to refine consciousness arises in the special training of thought and intent vis-à-vis consciousness. Once consciousness is formed, each time it reaches a certain level and a certain quality and quantity, the intent therein, which has already reached a degree of coordinated action, as well as part of vitality, energy, and spirit, still must undergo special training in "division," "interruption," and "combination," which proceed from thought and intent. The purpose of this training is to get the two constituents of consciousness to reach the level where they can separate and rejoin at any given time.

"Division" means to separate the intent from vitality, energy, and spirit, after they have already been conjoined and exercised in a coordinated manner so as to reach a highly developed level of refinement. This means causing them to redivide under the auspices of the new consciousness that has already been attained. This is like the force of action and reaction produced when an elastic object is expanded and compressed. This is called dividing yin and yang; yin and yang thus divided need to achieve the effect of mutual refinement in the process of their interaction.

"Interruption" means to interrupt or "cut apart" the intent and the vitality, energy, and spirit that are divided but not yet separated within consciousness. it means to interrupt the elastic connection between yin and yang, causing them to be independent, yet even in this independent condition still retain the special nature of coordinated action.

If we compare division to a series of conductors separately clustered at opposite poles of positive and negative charges, interruption can be likened to the electromagnetic phenomenon occurring in the gap. Here, the intent and the vitality, energy, and spirit divided in consciousness are separated, yet even under these conditions, where each is independent, they retain the coordinated ability to affect and respond to each other, and even to advance their mutual refinement a step.

There is an advanced step of interruption that is even more thoroughly penetrating. Suppose we say that after the previous step of interruption, there still exists, between intent and vitality, energy, and spirit, a consciousness field similar to an electromagnetic field; then this next step of interruption causes this field to be "turned off," so to speak, going from a manifest to an unmanifest state, transforming into a state of latency.

Here there appears an extremely special dynamic phenomenon (each level of consciousness and its division, interruption, and combination has its own dynamic effect): the action and reaction between intent and vitality, energy, and spirit in consciousness suddenly seems to disappear, yet the capacity proper to each of them does not really disappear at all. It is simply that the manifest relationship has been interrupted, retaining a latent, inward relationship that is very difficult for people to perceive.

Since the interaction of the yin and yang within consciousness has also disappeared (and there is no more distinction between yin and yang, so they have become the same, and yet each continues to undergo training while in a latent state), therefore the interaction between intent and consciousness disappears. These interactions only remain in thought, which does not demonstrate any physical effects. It is only with thought, furthermore, that one can ascertain the disappearance and appearance of these interactions.

The physical state of latency after thoroughgoing interruption has to be explained by means of metaphor and hypothesis. Suppose we grasp a leather strap ("consciousness") in both hands and pull it from both ends, stretching it tightly. The reaction in the hands of the elasticity of the leather corresponds to "division." If we soften the leather by physical or chemical means without changing the distance between the hands, then the elasticity changes a bit (corresponding to the first step of "interruption), and the power contained in the original elasticity is transferred to the hands. Now if we take a scissors to the softened leather, which still retains some elasticity, and cut through it (while the distance between the hands does not change), then the remaining bit of elastic tension will also be transferred to the hands, with no more power or force whatsoever remaining in the space between the two hands.

However, if that which stretches the leather strip (consciousness) tight is not a thing (hands) but rather "intent," then after the softening of the leather, the original elasticity (capacity, or power) falls partly into a void, although it is still connected through the softened leather strip. After completely cutting through it, the leather strip is divided into two pieces, with each releasing the power of its own elasticity, causing all of the elasticity to fall into a void. There being no connection, they do not manifest any action-reaction relationship.

The function and the power of intent on both sides thus also withdraw their total effective power. Then the two parts of elasticity (capacity) that have fallen into a void become formless "masses of capacity" imperceptible to ordinary people, and no longer interact.

Because they no longer interact, they are no longer manifest, and no longer contain distinctions between active and reactive force, meaning that they are neither yin nor yang. Because capacity keeps constant, therefore both masses of capacity are still actually there; because there is nowhere to transfer them, they "hang in the void." There being no function of intent, therefore they are highly independent; because they have a formless and forceless relationship with thought, therefore it is possible to control them only with thought. Being controlled by thought, they lose their antagonistic action-reaction relationship and assimilate to one another. That is why they can transform each other in the function of a single thought in action.

"Combination" has many forms; we will just cite three as examples. One kind is when thought takes the two masses of capacity and unites them into one body, combining them into a single mass of capacity, like two drops of water merging into one large drop. This can also be compared to an "assimilative field." The peculiarity of this "field" is that it can absorb any new yin and can also absorb any new yang. That is to say, whatever yin or yang power or force comes, from whatever direction, in each case the field has the ability to assimilate the force.

Another kind of combination is when thought restores, or re-manifests, the individual yin or yang nature of each mass of capacity. Alternatively, after transformation and reversal, thought may cause what was originally yin to turn into yang, cause what was originally yang to turn into yin, and at the same time change the original interaction between them, causing it to transform into unidirectional, unilaterally functioning power. This still involves thought merging the two masses of capacity into one, absorbing and unifying new yin and yang, then redividing yin and yang, and making them form a unidirectional function in concert. This produces a tremendous dynamic effect, potentiating an explosive power that cannot be resisted.

The third kind of combination is when thought causes the two masses of energy to follow their original route back to the source, becoming consciousness.

As we can see, division, interruption, and combination are actually only division and combination, because interruption is just a more advanced stage of division, a particular level of division.

The Foreground of Unification of Nature and Humanity

This sort of training of consciousness in division and combination is undoubtedly most thorough, profound, and exacting. The interplay of this training with the four major facets of the totality of the training, and the complex interactions among them, undoubtedly produce a very great influence. Supranormal training of consciousness produces a special supranormal consciousness, and also subjects the other major facets to supranormal training, so as to arrive at a supranormal level of physical and mental enhancement.

This multifaceted training of consciousness also creates a firm foundation for consciousness in its passive state. When consciousness has unified the totality of intent and vitality, energy, and spirit, the element of intent therein begins to gradually diminish, and there is a strengthening of the direct control of thought over vitality, energy, and spirit, until the element of intent recedes altogether. When the direct control of thought over the capacities of vitality, energy, and spirit reaches the appropriate level, then the task of intent is done. The first result of this is the merging of thought with vitality, energy, and spirit into one whole; this is the "mind" that is "single, undivided." This is what Buddhism calls "the mind unstained by even a mote of dust," the so-called original mind, or basic essential nature.

Only with this unified mind is it possible to exercise in coordination with the universe, and to receive, in the course of this coordinated exercise, a perpetual, ceaseless training. This is ever ongoing spontaneous enhancement by unminding cultivation of mind within the highest states of response of Nature to humanity, when Nature and humanity unite.

The foregoing is a general outline of one course of training, from consciously refining consciousness to spontaneity without conscious intent. Expressions such as "not applying intent, not applying effort," "consciousness without conscious intent is true consciousness," "emptiness," "the infinite," "unity," and so on, all allude to this supreme stage of training. The courses of training by which one may arrive at this are many and various, as already mentioned; the one introduced in this essay is just one kind.

CHAPTER 5

Refinement of Consciousness Is Not Solely in the Domain of Athletic Psychology

THE DISTINCTION BETWEEN the systems of traditional Chinese science and modern science have already been explained, in terms of their total scope and general concepts. From a literal point of view, the feeling conveyed to modern people by the word "consciousness" in the expression "refinement of consciousness" is that it refers to psychology, which investigates the domain of the psyche (or, in the context of movement and exercise, it is taken to refer to the psychology of athletics). In reality, however, the word "consciousness" here refers to a concept in which body and mind are indivisible. Use of the word "consciousness" to represent this mostly refers to a high level of conscious perception of the biological processes of the human body in movement, especially biodynamics.

In this sense, refinement of consciousness has a narrow meaning and a broad meaning. In its narrow meaning, we can only call it "supranormal biodynamic psychology." Not only does this include the corresponding parts of modern biodynamics and psychology; it refers to the total body-mind training peculiar to martial arts as it relates to the dynamics of the human body. It also makes special reference to the fact that "consciousness" in this sense is not the same as our ordinary fixed motivational structure or set of faculties.

The broad meaning includes the following:

1. Total omnifaceted training in enhanced conscious perception of the capacities of the human body and mind (which are of many

forms — physiology, biology, musculature, consciousness, energy, etc.)

2. The total dynamics, psychology, and process of the simplex and complex conditioned reflexes in the instinctive tensing that accompanies initiative and counterattack as well as overall movement, carrying out a course of re-recognition and reprocessing of these reflexes.

3. Training of the conscious perception of the dynamics of the human body peculiar to martial arts, which is "advanced dynamic thinking" with levels of awareness of physical movement and total awareness in action more advanced than what is recognized by relevant fields of modern science.

4. The physical and mental training involved in each system of support structure peculiar to martial arts.

5. Physical and mental discipline in the principles of fighting techniques, and disciplines of hygiene and health produced thereby.

And so on. The domain of the broad meaning of refinement of consciousness, other than the basic contents of ordinary psychology and the psychologies of human character, refers to the training of character peculiar to martial arts. This involves indivisible body-mind training of one's whole consciousness, whole psyche, and whole culture, through the courses and methods of martial arts. The training ultimately extends, furthermore, to the development of personality and will, as well as the highest character, philosophy, thought, and world view, as well as the highest level of morality and the highest realm of spiritual experience.

Based on the recognition of consciousness as a single entity in which mind and energy are fused, we cannot relegate refinement of consciousness to the psychology, physiology, or dynamics of exercise. We can only deal with it by viewing it as a triplex union of body, mind, and power. It has its own methods of training and direct experience, through which mind and body are simultaneously refined. It has its own modes of combining the structures and functions of physical and mental exercise. It has its own contents, with clearly distinct levels, having a very strong hologrammatic nature in each individual part. It has its own philosophical thought and methodology for guidance, and it has its own theory of cognition, simultaneously comprehending body and mind. To modern sciences dealing with the human body, it offers unique feedback from body-mind training, as well as a completely new angle and methodology for research.

After modern science finds out new methods of studying phenomena such as refinement of consciousness, and also obtains authentic results, this traditional Chinese science will also be sure to gain considerable feedback from that. Only thus can there take shape a situation amenable to creative research freely combining the ancient and the modern, the native and the foreign. And only then will there appear prospects for complementary progress of each way of thinking and angle of approach.

CHAPTER 6

Breakthroughs Associated with the Modality of Penetrating Power in Martial Arts

IT WOULD BE IMPOSSIBLE to fully expound the content of refinement of consciousness in high level martial arts with only one chapter of this book; this is an ideal to be realized only after multifaceted research by many scientists. All we can do is go through the particular levels, examples, and concepts pertaining to the broad and narrow meanings of refinement of consciousness as noted above, introducing the subject as best we can for the reader's reference, attempting to speak in modern terms.

At the same time, we still hope to be able to provide the reader with clues reflecting the whole picture, and we hope the reader will derive some sort of edification from it. In this section, we will begin our discussion with the topic of the manner of conducting and guiding force, or power.

Penetrating Power: A Special Method of Conduction of Power

Modern science dealing with the movement of the human body only recognizes muscular dynamics and conduction of force on the model of the lever. The human skeleton resembles a complex system of levers, with each lever, and the intervals between levers, having muscles that pull and regulate each other, fixed in place by tendons. Under the direction of the brain and the instincts, the muscles can produce movement by alternating tension and relaxation, thus together with the skeleton forming a complex moving structure. In this structure, the manner of transmission of power has the nature of mechanical dynamics.

For example, in the action of delivering a punch, as a result of the combined efforts of the whole body, a corresponding quantity of power is concentrated in the fist and applied to the point at which the blow is struck. But no matter how much training an athlete has, each of his joints disperses some force, either toward the inside or toward the outside of the body, thus creating a tremendous waste of muscular power. When exercise is done at a rapid pace, or for an extended continuous period of time, this sort of waste increases a hundredfold. It is because of this that the three elements of modern physical training are strength, speed, and endurance.

Chinese martial arts have made rarely recognized breakthroughs in the transmission and conduction of power. One kind of breakthrough in the mode of conduction is referred to by certain expressions used in pugilistic theory such as "one energy penetrating all the way through," "passing each joint in a continuum," and "traveling force." (There are, of course, also other types of transmission.) This mode retains the necessary elements of the manner of transmission of muscular force through a system of levers, yet brings out a penetrating mode of conduction by which it is possible to break through the limitations of each individual joint, thus greatly reducing the waste of muscular force created by ordinary methods.

The reader may ask, "How is this possible? A muscle can contract and relax; it is not possible for the same muscle to be contracted at one joint while relaxed at another joint. Furthermore, when a muscle alternately contracts and relaxes, in that capacity there is no possibility of transmission or conduction in the manner of liquid or gaseous dynamics."

This perception is based on modern anatomical knowledge; the perception of martial arts is otherwise. In martial arts, it has been discovered that the tension in muscles can be transmitted, conducted, and made to flow over long lines under the direction of thought or intent, either inch by inch or leaping through several joints at once. This is the "traveling" in "traveling force." When the tension at one point is transferred an inch further along, then this point can relax. Furthermore, this is not limited by any anatomical structure (such as bone joints or muscular and ligament structures). Accordingly, every fiber of the human body, and totality of the body, becomes a conductor of power, just as metal is a conductor of electricity, and a pipe is a conductor of water.

One of the basic exercises for refinement of consciousness also starts from precisely this point. So many people have made consciousness into something mysterious and inconceivable, viewing it as a supernatural phenomenon that cannot be understood by common sense. In reality, consciousness in this context is no more than a result of ordinary consciousness going through this sort of training to exert a more advanced degree of control over motor capacity.

This is the starting point, the foundation of consciousness. This is where martial arts part ways with other physical exercises. When one advances level by level on this path, from proficiency to skill, from skill to genius, to the point where one is enabled to actually sense the unfathomable, this is in accord with the same natural principle of any highly advanced technology or art when it is at a level where it is on the vanguard of development and manifests the phenomenon of going beyond genius into the quintessence of creativity.

Without analysis by thought and propulsion and direction by will, the conduction of muscular tension over long lines leaping past joints and ligaments is not possible. This is because muscular tension in the process of normal conditioned response (that is, in the process of motor response after having received the command of consciousness) is not subject to conscious control. And it is precisely the interaction of intent with this kind of penetrating transmission, passing through joint after joint without being subjected to limitation by joints and tendons, that produces the crude consciousness merged in union with vitality, energy, and spirit (meaning, in this context, muscular power).

Once you have this kind of consciousness, then muscular tension can be likened to a pearl rolling along a pipeline, coursing through the human body as if through a system of wires or pipes. It can also form a complete line of elasticity penetrating from the feet through to the hands, without dispersing power at the joints or ligaments.

This sort of transmission of power not only takes place in one's own body; it can also be transmitted to the body of another, under the control of one's own will. Furthermore, even then it still remains obedient to the control of one's own will, in a state difficult for the other to notice (the body and mind of the ordinary person do not recognize this kind of phenomenon).

Once you are like this, however, your dynamic structure is no longer a simple combination of levers and transmission systems. There is a change in the supporting structure and the transference of power, brought on by a new transmission system. This results in the formation of a twofold dynamic structure for support and transmission of power. These two structures can also exchange and combine functions.

One can also cause similar changes to occur, furthermore, in the bodies of others, even against their will. This produces a state of affairs where the individual acting as the motive force is unknown as such to others, being the only one who knows people's true condition. This is a kind of situation where a person causes others to have no choice but submit to the motivation without knowing why.

The combining of intent and vitality-energy-spirit (now meaning muscular tension and relaxation) involved in training this kind of transmission is actually an important preliminary step in the aforementioned training in advanced conscious perception of the capacities of the human body and mind.

Because here conscious perception, through a certain method, penetrates deeply into that part of the domain of control over muscular tension and relaxation that is ordinarily not subject to deliberate conscious control, it creates a mode of transmission of consciousness in which two things are merged into one (intent and power are coordinated).

Once the human body has been transformed into a conductor, then power can be transmitted to the body of another and caused to flow according to one's own will. This ability greatly expands the range of the dynamic structure and capacity for exerting force in the human body. It also elevates the degree of independence in the active employment of power. At the same time, this is a stage in the whole process of combined refinement of consciousness and the body at which it is comparatively easy to perceive how this special capacity of consciousness is formed.

A Special Mode of Conduction: Results and Prospects

The contents of this subsection can only be generalized, because the issues touched upon are extremely complex. Nevertheless, without some explanation, there is no way to make the connection with the material to follow.

The crude consciousness explained above has to go through many levels of training, advancing higher stage by stage, until a certain kind of qualitative transformation takes place. This is consciousness (which, it will be remembered, is a combination of consciousness and power) that can be conducted through the space between one's own body and the body of another, thus becoming a kind of indefinable potential provided by a system that continually expands and releases the effective function of the structural dynamics and energetic force of the human body.

In martial arts, when we speak of penetrating power, or force emanating from the hands, or forceful energy escaping the physical body, or "consciousness reaching, energy reaching, force reaching," all of these expressions refer to the fact that power can be conducted outside the body along with consciousness.

The force of consciousness can pass through and beyond the human body, and can even act and transmute in space after liberation from the limitations of the physical structure of the human body. This is an extraordinary phenomenon peculiar to martial arts and energetics.

Previously we have explained how consciousness still needs to go through many levels of training in division, interruption, and combination. There is, furthermore, the action of thought on consciousness effected through intent; and there is also the direct action of thought on consciousness. Adding the power of the force of consciousness inside and outside the human body, it is possible to form a variety of "consciousness fields."

Based on this, it is possible for consciousness, with the cooperative action of thought or thought plus intent, to create at will a formless consciousness field that can be deliberately controlled. It is also possible to evoke a corresponding dynamic effect, which could be called a field effect.

When a human body that has been made into a conductor of power transmits (or releases) that power into a space, this power is no longer subject to the limitations of the structure of the conductor. Furthermore, in the course of a certain process it departs from the medium of a solid body and an electric body (i.e. the human body), thus coming under the direct control of conscious thought.

When this power reaches open space, then it is "energy." It could also be called a field of consciousness and energy, which is thus a field of conscious energy, or the energy of consciousness. This can be concentrated and dispersed, and can create a formless point, line, plane, or body; it can take on any mode of movement and spatial dimension desired. Furthermore, in the context of elevating one's own powers of response to the environment and concrete application to martial arts and health, it activates a field effect that has practical usefulness.

The reason that modern science finds it extremely difficult to study this phenomenon, aside from fundamental methodological problems, is that present-day techniques of brain science have not yet developed to a level where they can measure the various levels of interaction among thought, intent, consciousness, and vitality-energy-spirit. The computer is not sensitive enough for this task; the essential nature of consciousness has not been made explicit; and the essential nature of energy has not been clarified. Although some phenomena have been verified as realities, no explanation has been found within the scope of modern scientific theories. It is truly a case of "a dog trying to bite a porcupine but finding no way to get its teeth in."

Nevertheless, the existence of these very difficulties and contradictions has created a premise for a revolutionary change in science as a whole. Sooner or later, during and after this revolution, science will produce for mankind an unprecedented contribution, perhaps its greatest ever: to reveal the inner mysteries of human life and thought.

CHAPTER 7

"The Last to Act Overcomes Others" and Conditioned Reflexes

E ACH SUBSCHOOL OF martial arts has its own technical principles and methods of combat. Some emphasize "using offense for defense," some emphasize "using defense for offense."

The principle of offensive and defensive fighting most familiar to people is to set up conditions favorable to initiating aggressive offense; this is the principle of struggling for precedence. Within the domain of combat in the ordinary sense, this is an effective enough way to resolve practical problems and obtain results in emergencies.

When martial arts reach a relatively high level, however, then problems are handled by addressing potentials and momenta. This core principle of potential and momentum is expressed by the saying, "The last to act overcomes others."

What Is the Meaning of "The Last to Act Overcomes Others"?

Unlike the principle of aggressive initiative and struggle for precedence, the technical principle of the last to act overcoming others places emphasis on the need to have opponents make the first move. There are three related misunderstandings, or biased views, which have to be cleared up.

One is the idea that "the last to act overcomes others" means letting opponents throw the first blows, countering only after an opponent has thrown several punches. Another is the idea that this is the moral or ethical principle of deference, letting opponents throw the first blows to show that you have no aggressive intention of your own. The third is that this sort of deference is actually proof that you have the mastery and power to seize victory, since only someone who is strong has the capability and the qualifications to allow others to lash out.

We consider all three of these views to be biased and thus alienated from the real nature and original meaning of "the last to act overcomes others." Speaking from the angle of techniques for seizing victory, the idea of first waiting for opponents to launch several blows is unreasonable, no matter how you interpret it. Self-preservation, avoiding injury, and overcoming adversaries are fundamental principles of martial arts fighting techniques. Even if allowing an opponent to make the first move is an ordinary way of feeling the opponent out, enabling you to find out his relative attainment and strength, and thus break up his offensive and seize victory, this is certainly not because of "deference."

One's own power and mastery, furthermore, do not need to be proven by allowing opponents to launch several blows first; they are more evident in the techniques employed to overcome opponents.

When advanced martial artists are definitely far superior to opponents, they have the capability to defend themselves, and also to overcome opponents without actually injuring them. When it comes to "the last to act overcomes others" in the authentic sense, the strategy of allowing an opponent to make the first move is technically and theoretically in conformity with the requirements of the principle of nonaggression, yet the one does not follow from the other.

Of course, this conformity enables ethical and technical principles to attain harmony and unity, so that ethical standards have the powerful support of technical principles, thus forming the essential part of martial arts and the training of human character. This is what is most valuable and meaningful in the finest tradition of advanced martial arts.

It is only after this sort of breakthrough, which enables martial arts to develop to its highest levels, that we can dare to say that pugilistic technique in itself is a minor art. This creates the technical and ethical basis for the self-transcending transition of martial arts from pugilistics to the search for the Tao.

Then what, after all, is the basic meaning of the principle "the last to act overcomes others"? The point is to allow the opponent to act first, to make the first move (or first activate the intention to make a move), so as to enable you to have an opportunity to discern the opponent's emptiness or fullness, after which you take advantage of a gap to get in there and seize victory.

This principle is relatively easy to explain in terms of ordinary logic. As long as the bodies and minds of both sides have not moved, both are in a sort of static state of equilibrium. Whoever makes the first move thereby first breaks this equilibrium; moreover, he first breaks his own equilibrium, thus revealing his own flaw, giving his opponent an opportunity that can be exploited.

But what are the theoretical, technical, and pragmatic foundations of the ability to take advantage of a gap to gain access to an opponent, shifting from a passive to an active mode?

To address this problem, martial arts have developed a number of tactical principles and corresponding techniques whereby "the last to act overcomes others." We will choose one of them as an example, to explain how this principle is not at all a matter of first waiting for the opponent to launch three blows, as so many people think, then making a counterattack.

The fundamental issue we are discussing here, however, lies in a basic distinction. In modern pugilistic sports, there is also the principle and actual phenomenon of "the last to set out arriving first." This is a sort of superhuman capacity based on strengthening the speed of conditioned reflexes. In the martial arts we are discussing, in contrast, "the last to set out is the first to arrive" is a kind of very special inviolable principle.

The theoretical and pragmatic basis of this principle treats ordinary conditioned reflex with a kind of special processing that also contains the practical design of the comprehensive routines of martial arts.

In order to explain how this type of processing is different from, and superior to, processing based on conditioned reflex, we have to recognize, from a completely new angle, the basic mechanical limitations and deficiencies of conditioned reflex in the context of pugilism. Then we can talk about how martial arts can overcome or exploit these deficiencies and reach a degree of speed unattainable by conditioned reflex (no matter how highly trained), whereby it is possible to gain the mastery and control to face ordinary conditioned reflex and "prevail first by acting last."

"Leakage" in Conditioned Reflex

First of all, we will make a crude "slow motion camera" outline analysis of the basic "cell" of the offensive and defensive exercise of attack and response.

1. Attack

The one who launches an attack must first activate intention (here we omit the various judgments and other preliminaries of activating intention). Activating intention means the brain sends a command to the muscles. This command includes a complete plan of action, from the point of initiation through the route of movement to its aim. It includes various anticipated effects, such as the physical resistance when you strike an opponent, the physical configuration and dynamic relationship into which both parties are thereby locked, the destruction of the opponent's equilibrium and the maintenance (or restoration) of one's own equilibrium. Of course, it also includes the quantity of stimulation delivered to the musculature, which is a specific amount of capacity needed to meet the necessary expenditure, and so on. (Some of the detailed physiological, biological, and psychological processes discussed in this chapter still await research.)

After volition has sent its command and mobilized the muscles, then one can only await the result. Depending on whether the result is good or bad, one creates a new decision through conscious or subconscious judgment, transmitting another command. Thus is formed a continuous cycle of mobilization of intent, motor activity, judgment of results, decision, remobilization of intent, and so on.

Each time the muscles move, each time they receive a command, if they do not complete their whole function then it is not possible for there to be any discrete action. Muscles act on the basis of the rules of ordinary conditioned reflex; they themselves have no "brains" in the process of each reflex, and they cannot "think" either. Unless there is a result, connecting to a new command (or there is the stimulus of an opponent's parry or blow), the muscles cannot act on their own. Under conditions where they are disconnected from consciousness, or before they have received any new stimulus, they do not have the power to change the route of movement or present a new plan of action.

What is even more important is that in the course of the total process, after the muscles receive the command and before the result is fed back to the brain, during that interval the consciousness loses its "directing authority" over the musculature. The process of motor reflex is not subject to the control of consciousness; before the reflex process is completed, consciousness has no power to affect it.

It is clearly evident that consciousness and muscles act alternately over time, and in the process of action they combine in an alternating manner. In a continuous series of movements, even though it is possible to take several actions and combine them into one single action, nevertheless from the point of view of the whole body the nature of this alternation does not change. Each movement involves a process from the activation of consciousness to the activation of the musculature, a process from the beginning to the conclusion of a motor action, and a process of the resulting response to each action being fed back to the brain.

These three processes are irreversible; there is no way to change them in mid-route. Only after the conclusion of these three processes can the individual's consciousness make a judgment (the fourth process) based on the final results of this action, determine a plan of followup action (the fifth process), transmit this plan to intent (the sixth process), which finally can initiate a new activation of consciousness.

Leaving aside yet more subtle conditions, as long as the person does not relinquish consciousness of attack and defense, between every two movements of consciousness there are altogether six irreversible processes, which cannot be changed by will.

To sum up, in each action of the body and mind, volition sends a command but does not "participate in the battle." It is the musculature that "participates in battle." However, in the course of the total process of participation in an action, before a new command comes down the act is not under the control of consciousness. Modern athletic and pugilistic training are only capable of enhancing the "elements" of the whole process from one activation of consciousness to the next activation of consciousness, such as the speed of the whole six processes, the liveliness of adaptation in the judgment and plan of action, whether thinkingly or subconsciously, muscular strength and overall endurance. Nevertheless, they have no way at all to reduce any one of these processes.

When skill in one exercise is perfected, and technical ability reaches the level of conscious control, some of the processes can be eliminated by chance. This represents the peak level manifested in the body-mind constitution and athletic technique of advanced athletes in modern times. This has, however, a considerable measure of accidental "sparks of genius," a kind of inspired state not under the individual's own control. It is not a result of a systematic grasp of the principles of cultivating this sort of inspired state.

2. Response

Another constituent of this attack-response "cell" is the reactive movement of one party. This response may take the form of counterattack, blocking, slipping, or dodging, but in any case it is in the same category of response or reaction. The nature of this action is the same as that of the action of the attacker.

3. Judgment and Decision

Between the actions of both sides, there is an individual judgment of both one's own and the adversary's condition and movement. This judgment is the acquisition and processing of ongoing information, before and after acting, of the results of the action. The process of judgment (which for now will all be assigned to the fourth process included in all actions, as noted above) is one that takes time; it is also subdivided into a number of subprocesses, such as the gathering of information through the eyes, ears, and the body (the sense of physical motion), and the comprehensive processing of this information; then producing a continuous cycle between an intention and a new plan (a new intention). On the basis of judgment, intention, and decision, there may also appear problems of conflict and choice between two (or more) relatively objective and relatively subjective conditions; this also requires a certain amount of time to complete.

To summarize, the nature and peculiarity of every action based on ordinary conditioned reflexes is that it causes the superiority or inferiority of both parties, their victory or defeat, to be completely determined by each individual's strength, speed, endurance, agility, athletic skill, technical ability, accuracy of judgment and planning, as well as the alternation and combination of the mental and the physical, including the power of the cooperative effort.

Our idea of recognizing the basic mechanical limitations and deficiencies of conditioned reflex in the context of pugilism approaches the matter from the angle of coordination of consciousness and the body, regarding the six processes between each activation of consciousness and the next (including the consumption of time and energy) as being in principle deficiencies and leakages that can be eliminated. And these processes can only be brought to light and shown to be deficiencies and leakages when compared to the cognitive and technical management characteristic of true psychophysical coordination. This is what we call the re-recognition and reprocessing of conditioned reflex.

From Simultaneous Refinement of Consciousness and the Body to Psychophysical Coordination

Starting out from our own angle of approach, using our own theoretical and practical methods, dealing with the defect of the disjunction of consciousness and the body in conditioned reflex, and thus finding rules and methods of overcoming this defect, is a great contribution of Chinese martial arts to the sciences of human movement and exercise, and by extension to the whole science of the human body. The theory and methodology of martial arts have already been discussed; in terms of concrete procedure, what is involved is going from simultaneous refinement of consciousness and the body to psychophysical coordination.

The lessons and contributions of martial arts to the fundamental theories of the science of the human body are certainly not limited to this, but even on this basis alone it can be predicted that with the full disinterment, systematization, translation, and advanced research in martial arts, they will be able to induce a profoundly revolutionary change in modern sciences of athletic and physical education, indeed even in the whole range of science of the human body.

Through the foregoing discussions on traditional theories, on consciousness, on using consciousness to refine consciousness, on the breakthrough of penetrating force, and so on, we have already gained an elementary perception of simultaneous refinement of consciousness and the body, and of refinement of consciousness itself. Here we will proceed to a simple explanation of the course of training from simultaneous refinement of consciousness and the body to psychophysical coordination, and how to overcome the deficiencies and leakage of conditioned reflex.

In order to set forth a fundamental distinction, and in order to produce the clearest description of the results of coordination, we will begin by bringing out the highest aim.

Viewed from the highest level of psychophysical coordination, that is, from the point of view of unity without duality, conditioned reflex is completely extinguished. Even if this sounds like an inconceivable abstract ideal, yet it is the highest goal of martial arts.

Speaking in terms of the total value of martial arts, this is nearly all-inclusive; here we will just pursue one thread, that of pugilism.

The representative principle of pugilism in its highest state is that neither party, oneself nor one's opponent, has any room at all to think or act. That is to say, there is fundamentally no way for either side to make the first move. Because in this realm the aforementioned six processes of conditioned reflex have all been eliminated, both parties are completely coordinated; no matter which one arouses the thought of moving a hand, the other one will use the power of coordinated intuitive response to cause him to relinquish this thought. Thus neither side has any way to move a hand; in other words, the equilibrium of the state before any action is launched cannot be broken.

Now let us skip over several stages, coming down from the highest level to one that has already been demonstrated by a few martial artists of the present day, in order to explain the results of simultaneous refinement of consciousness and the body.

A minor fruit of penetrating power is that one's own consciousness field enables one to respond swiftly to an opponent's force field. This includes a response to the opponent's movement of consciousness, which is used to make a coordinate response of one's own movement of consciousness to that of the opponent. The degree of coordination here is lower than that of the peak level mentioned before, but it is still much higher than the level of alternating cooperation of consciousness and the body in conditioned reflex.

The movement or activation of consciousness here refers to the intent of both parties. The result of the response is a coordination of one's own movement of consciousness with that of the other side. At the same time, one's own consciousness, that is to say consciousness in which intent and power are combined into one, is coordinated with one's own activation of consciousness as well as with the other side's activation of consciousness. As a result, one's own power is coordinated with the other side's movement of consciousness, whereas the other side's power and activation of consciousness are not coordinated, but rather alternate. Since the speed of coordination is greater by far than that of alternation, one can thereby preempt even a subtle movement by the other side. The subtle movement is consciousness, while preemption refers to one's own power acting before the other's power can act. Herein lies the theoretical and practical key to the principle that "the last to act overcomes others."

Psychophysical coordination is not an absolute coordination, but is subject to the limitations of the level of achievement in simultaneous refinement of consciousness and the body. With each advancing stage of refinement, it is possible to contract, or even overcome (extinguish) one of the six processes in conditioned reflex, so the speed of response can be made a step faster. When this refinement has been raised to a certain level, opponents no longer have the power even to renew activation of consciousness; that is, they are beaten the moment they stir their consciousness, with fundamentally no need for you to send a command to the musculature.

In pugilistic theory, this is called "finding people out before they have acted out." In other words, when an opponent is just about to launch a blow, you have already hit him before he has even moved a hand.

When you have advanced several steps beyond this, you deal directly with the opponent's activation or movement of consciousness. This is using consciousness to oppose consciousness, in which case there is fundamentally no need even to move the hands.

Beginning with the so-called penetrating power or penetrating force, the human body is transformed into a conductor, until one can even conduct the forceful power outside one's own body, to the degree where it forms a metamorphosing extracorporeal consciousness field that obey's one's will, with actual dynamic effects. And through this consciousness field one affects the action of opponents' consciousness, after which one then gradually elevates the level of one's ability to move in step with an opponent, until one reaches an altogether different stage, where the basic response mechanism does not operate by means of physical movement, but by "field effect." This is the step-by-step developmental process from simultaneous refinement of consciousness and the body to psychophysical coordination.

This is a good example of how we use the theory and practice of simultaneous refinement of consciousness and the body to carry out re-recognition and reprocessing of conditioned reflex. It is also a classic example of how we can use the principles of martial arts and the fruits of classical philosophy to study modern science and its achievements. At the same time, it is also a sort of experiment in translating ancient theories into modern language.

If both martial arts and science can accept interactive research and cooperative progress as a guiding ideology, and establish conditions for conceptualization and dialogue based on mutual study, using each other as examples and as tools, and thus establish a relationship of equality and mutual assistance in which both sides are scientific researchers collaborating in research on every sort of topic, equally enjoying the fruits of scientific research, if they can collectively accept and recognize the principle that the fruits of scientific research belong to both sides, then there is the possibility for actualizing an ideal cooperative effort. Only then can there be a really effective positivity bringing out the best in both, and a highly efficient creative development pushing the study of martial arts in a forward direction.

Why Softness Can Overcome Hardness

"The last to act, the first to take control" and "finding people out before they act out" use the principle of psychophysical coordination to resolve the problem of speed. The reason these modes can "overcome hardness by softness" is that they also have extra-ordinary solutions for problems such as strength and endurance. This is still based on the principle of psychophysical coordination.

To begin with, the mode of training used by advanced martial arts for the simultaneous refinement of consciousness and the body is, above all, one that resolves problems of strength and endurance through the avenue of modulation of capacity. Quite clearly, the course from "penetrating power" to "field effect" is one of gradually enhanced ability to moderate capacity. When you get to the stage when you do battle by pitting consciousness against consciousness, what is employed is "consciousness," which is extremely light and extremely fine; so where is there any expenditure of motor capacity consuming strength?

Even when you are still using muscular strength (consciousness in which intent and muscular power are combined), you still absolutely employ the principle of "borrowing strength," where you use an opponent's force to strike the opponent. Your vital energy is only used to array a "consciousness field" causing the opponent to fall into a situation where he is made to act in such a way that he cancels himself out by himself, either falling into a void or hitting himself, while you remain extremely relaxed and reserved.

When an opponent has fallen into a state where he does not know what to do, and is fully vulnerable to being influenced, if it is still necessary for you to strike him, your forceful power, which can be made to flow according to will, is able to fire off a totally concentrated, high velocity, high power blast, exercising a devastating capacity that is likened to "throwing stones down a well." What is employed here is a highly orderly "consciousness" that does not give rise to any of the sort of waste brought on by any kind of dispersal of power.

Because you are last to act, because you let the opponent make the first move, you remain in a highly relaxed state, "awaiting action in stillness," while your mind is extraordinarily steady. There is not the slightest element of tension in you, and you do not break your own equilibrium with any subjective action at all. Thus minimizing the expenditure of mental and physical capacity to the greatest possible limit, you can often accomplish with one quantum of capacity what would ordinarily take a hundred, or a thousand, or even ten thousand times as much capacity to achieve.

There is no new principle of dynamics here at all; no change at all takes place in the principles of dynamics. All that has changed is the field effect brought on by penetrating power, and the structure of the consciousness field. The effect of overcoming the hard by means of softness is an immutable principle, which is realized under the conditions of psychophysical coordination and the resulting field effect.

Using the principle of coordination in modulation of capacity, field effect, and superiority of speed, at the same time we can gain a special endurance that comes from this. Under conditions of extreme speed, extreme relaxation, and extreme minimization of effort, even the endurance of an average person can far exceed that of a modern athlete.

Let us reflect on this for a moment. Without special techniques for speed, modulation of capacity, and explosive power created through modulation of capacity, how can we interpret the actual fact that the weak can overcome the strong, using softness to prevail over hardness? If not for psychophysical coordination, and the field effect thus produced, how can we interpret "power traveling through space," or the phenomenon of striking someone from a distance? How can we explain the matter of experts being able to distinguish someone's level of ability without a single move being made, without any contact?

Using martial arts to study modern science, we can pose questions that science cannot pose; through mutual comparison, it is possible to produce explanations that science cannot, thus making it possible to present new ways of thinking and new directions for scientific study, making new experiments within the range accessible to modern science. Only thus can we hope to clarify certain issues from a modern point of view.

Only when martial arts and science are accorded equal status in this way, interacting on a basis of equality, will they be able to realize mutual stimulation to progress. Research based only on the fixed viewpoint and methodology of science, leaving out the results and methodology of martial arts themselves, can hardly be successful.

The foregoing section, in addition to introducing the concepts of martial arts and seeking to interpret some of the phenomena associated with refinement of consciousness, also proposes a truly rational relationship between martial arts and science.

So, having probed the three elements of modern training, let us ask what methods martial arts use to train their own three elements.

CHAPTER 8

The Laboratory of Refinement of Consciousness

T HE PECULIARITY OF the methodology of martial arts lies in this: in the process of simultaneous refinement of consciousness and the body, using consciousness to refine consciousness, practitioners of martial arts go through a course of simultaneous awakening of body and mind to elevate their own levels of realization. This is a kind of science that requires one to make oneself the object of research. The subjective and objective being are one's own body and mind, the total body-mind; no particular part is singled out. The laboratory, the object of experimentation, the experimenter, and the equipment used in the experiment, are all oneself.

In the process of simultaneous awakening of body and mind, there is analysis, and also synthesis; but even when concretely analyzing a certain part, this part still retains its living interactive function within the totality of the whole body-mind system. When there is synthesis (that is, when there is a so-called awakening), no matter what kind of abstract order is produced, this order must simultaneously function in every part of the whole, including and combining each and every part, preserving the reality of each part. That is to say, in this kind of special scientific research, the abstract never loses its concrete sensibility, while the concrete never loses its realistic relationship with the whole.

Regarding the recognition of the structure of movement and the total mechanical limitations of each individual action, this also requires many repeated experiments. Recognition here refers, first of all, to recognition of the phenomenon of consciousness and the body escaping limitations. This means going through a cognitive process leading from having no way of mastery to finding a way to mastery, then proceeding to analyze the abundant theoretical and practical material gained through simultaneous awakening of body and mind, seeking to master the natural laws of this contradiction, including the favorable conditions and hidden powers of the human body and brain.

Reprocessing refers to the concrete process of mastering this contradiction. That includes fostering new elements of thought and consciousness, new awareness of stillness and movement, new structures of physical action, new expressions of synthesis, new capacities of compensation and replenishment in exercise, new advanced total awareness of movement, a new sense of self-defense, and so on. In other words, it refers to the various concrete measures and methods used to develop a new physical and mental constitution.

The "Specimen," or Object of Experimentation

When modern science researches subatomic or high velocity phenomena, for the sake of convenience in doing research, whatever can be magnified is first magnified, and whatever can be slowed down is slowed down. For example, a specimen may be placed under a high power microscope, or an event may be photographed at high speed and then replayed in slow motion, or other artificial means may be used to achieve slow motion. By guaranteeing that the nature of the specimen and the life process does not change, and getting rid of extraneous elements that might cause disturbance, strict experimental conditions are more easily assured.

We cannot help admiring the intelligence of the ancient Chinese people: even before the existence of modern scientific knowledge, technology, and instrumentation, in the techniques and principles of martial arts, that is, in the structural analysis and reprocessing of each action of the human body, by their own methods they attained special miracles of scientific research that have never yet been discovered, resolved, or explained by countless modern sciences.

Martial arts flash past the process of conditioned reflex with the speed of lightning. It is as though the process had been placed under a microscope, artificially enlarged and slowed down to such a high degree as to enable people to obtain the necessary preliminary conditions for detailed perception and investigation of the process, namely a suitable specimen for experimentation.

The conditions for a specimen are quite exacting. The construction of a specimen is itself a specific technique, which thus must be studied. In this case, the specimen is the functional structure and dynamic process of a movement or action. The necessary conditions are strictly circumscribed by the need for a high degree of reduction in speed, plus a high degree of magnification, so as to ensure that the particular process of any given movement or action (that is, any conditioned reflex) has all of its necessary elements, preserving their integrity intact. Furthermore, at every point in the course of movement, even at a point when in a state of surface stillness, it is also necessary to ensure that the whole process is present within the totality of the psychological and dynamic elements of action involved at this particular point.

Be it the moment just before consciousness is activated, or the moment that power has gone into motion but has not yet reached its terminus, or the moment power is just about to reach its terminus, or the moment of just having struck an opponent but not having finished striking, or the moment before striking an opponent when you are therefore about to lose control over your equilibrium but have not yet really lost it, in each case it is necessary to slow down and magnify the moment in order to make sure of all the elements of action at normal speed. The items mentioned here are just simple examples of one part of each "specimen."

Thus the construction of the specimen itself is a single basic exercise of martial arts. Enhancement of the level of the construction, furthermore, is determined by the collective enhancement of each basic exercise. Quite clearly, the experimental specimen is a specific process of movement or action of the human body and mind.

The Experimenter and the Instrumentation

As mentioned earlier, the experimenter and the instrumentation are also the human body and mind. It is the human body and mind that carry out the analysis, synthesis, and cognition of each change in the specimen, including changes in all modes of capacity—biological, kinetic, and psychological—in the simultaneous awakening of body and mind.

This process is made highly conscious; the individual's conscious perception enters deeply into a domain it has never before experienced, such as the parts of the process of instinctive tensing and conditioned reflex that have never before been subject to conscious control. The instruments used in experimentation are thought, intent, and consciousness.

"Input Power" and the Comprehension of Simultaneous Awakening of Body and Mind

Input power (also called the input phenomenon) is a teacher's method of instruction, guidance, testing, and evaluation in an experiment. The student presents a specimen, then works on comprehension and assessment of physical and mental changes in the course of the teacher's "input maneuvering."

This means that students must mobilize all of their intelligence (methods of comprehension, logical and alogical reasoning, the total sensory system, understanding, and intuition) in order to minutely discern the various subtle movements of thought and inner power on both sides, including the various changes that take place in the level of movement of thought, using the simultaneous awakening of body and mind to understand and absorb the experience.

Going on through many kinds of methods, including simple exercises, footwork, fistwork, use of apparatus, paired practice, and so on, progressing in absorption and mastery of what is learned, repeating over and over again, the process of stage by stage elevation ultimately reaches a level where one experiences a sense of total communion and penetration. This is the intensely conscious experimental process of simultaneous refinement of consciousness and the body to the point where psychophysical coordination is attained.

The verbal instruction and mental input of the teacher is indispensable. It is essential to have a teacher; it is necessary to go through physical and mental contact with a teacher and fellow students. Simply relying on "book knowledge" and individual practice does not work. Just as a swimmer must make contact with water, it is necessary to have contact with a teacher before it is possible to proceed with the endless process of individual absorption of the teachings. Only then can one learn advanced martial arts. As it is said, "The way into the gate requires oral instruction; the principle of practice unceasing is cultivated by oneself."

Through mutual research of martial arts and science, it may be that some of the steps involved in this training could be compressed, or even eliminated; the whole process could be speeded up. Nevertheless, it will be necessary to go through this unavoidable route of the feeding maneuver; there is no way to change this. The function of the teacher's feed-in action is the function of matching the model specimen and the student's specimen.

Swimmers realize and train their own swimming ability from the power of interaction between themselves and the water. Students of martial arts learn to recognize interactive and reactive relations through "hearing power" from a teacher and appropriate feeding actions or maneuvers. In the course of nonordinary reaction, furthermore, they come to learn to distinguish the difference between ordinary and extra-ordinary functions.

Only after students have grasped new methods of thinking and principles of training, only after they have learned extra-ordinary techniques, are they then able to be creative, based on the peculiarities of the structure of their knowledge and the constitution of their bodies and minds. The enlightenment of an enlightened teacher lies in the ability to transmit one and the same unchanging technical foundation to students of different characteristics. It is necessary for the teacher to use dissimilar materials to produce the same product, and then after that to teach students to develop their individual strengths on their own.

Higher Conscious Perception

Higher conscious perception is the transformation of motor activity into consciousness, and the transformation of consciousness into motor activity (or into power), through the interaction and mutual reconstruction of the musculature and consciousness.

The most recent research has proven that muscles also have their own consciousness and memory, called muscular consciousness and muscular memory. The aim of martial arts includes maximum development and strengthening of muscular consciousness and memory, so as to enable these two elements to exercise their special responsive functions after conscious intent has gradually withdrawn.

As stated above, psychophysical coordination means that consciousness and the body no longer disconnect with the constitutional changes involved in each movement or action. Thought and intent are no longer simply commanding officers giving out orders and examining the results of battle; they are warriors directly involved in battle from start to finish, working in unison, combining their power without interruption.

Because of this, consciousness can adjust the plan of action, the route of movement of power, and the target, at any time in the total process of the exercise of power, causing power to always have a "brain" that can "think" throughout the course of the whole process. By this means one attains the adaptive capability and strategic autonomy to coordinate action and response with opponents. One attains, moreover, a technical guarantee of one hundred percent victory against attacks that are based on conditioned reflex, no matter how swift they may be. This is referred to as "knowing others yet being unknown to others."

The interactive function and mutual reconstruction that take place in the mutual refinement of consciousness and the body do not alternate, regardless of the state and subjective feeling of the individual; they are carried on in a coordinated manner. From this we can realize what special abilities can be developed by such an in-depth and systematic training, such as a strong will, advanced awareness of movement, and special powers of concentration.

CHAPTER 9

Training Dynamic Thought and Higher Apperception

Such a penetrating training of body and mind cannot but reflect on the domain of thought. When someone's whole system of awareness of movement, the existing system of total awareness of movement plus the conscious perception of movement, goes through this sort of complete overhaul, this can open up a new universe in the person's realm of thought. This new universe is higher than the results of any sort of modern training of expression, imagination, or thought; it is higher than any sort of psychological training such as relaxation, self-control, suggestion, and so on. We call it dynamic high-level thinking, or "dynamic thinking."

Readers may already be accustomed to our use of the point of view of unification of body and mind. Dynamic thinking, similarly, is a particular kind of thought, a direct activity of the brain. At the same time, it is also a kind of power, which has dynamic effects. In order to elucidate this issue, we have to borrow the fruits of modern psychology of speech. Of course, we will only touch upon those aspects that relate to our main topic of refinement of consciousness, and we will only introduce generalities. So there is a certain bias in this usage, which is after all only a borrowing.

External Speech and Internal Speech

There may be those who are as yet unaware that the formation of our thinking capacity is inseparable from motor activity. This is an essential point, not to be overlooked when we discuss the issue of dynamic thought.

When we are small children, each of us has to go through a developmental stage of intuitive action and thought. In this stage, the whole process of our movement, feeling, seeing, hearing, and so on, is inseparable from motor activity. This is common knowledge. The learning of language, furthermore, in infancy and childhood, including the lifelong capacity for verbal communication, is inseparable from the sound-producing organs, which participate in the process of speech—the respiratory system, lips and teeth, the tongue, the upper and lower jaws, the vocal cords, and the related hearing and seeing systems. Among these, those over which control is trained are mainly the muscles of the voice-producing system and the related aural and visual systems.

This is a kind of training in control of the interaction between consciousness and the musculature. This process is not easily understood by those who have not gone through special training. Everyone can remember personal childhood experiences, can observe other children, and can also refer to experiences of foreign language leaning in adulthood; thus it is possible to review this training process from a new angle.

The speech of children develops by imitation of adults. This includes imitation of individual sounds, groups of sounds, individual words, groups of words, short and long phrases, and ultimately interlinking statements. In order to produce intelligible sounds conveying meaning, the muscular structures of our voice-producing organs undergo an extremely complex and difficult long-term training. This training is accompanied throughout by a complex process in which are combined vocabulary, concepts, grammar, logic, symbolism, the circumstances of communication, and the psychological states of those involved. Only thus does verbal intercourse become possible, enabling people to understand what others say, and to speak in a manner that others can understand, thus producing an exchange of ideas.

This is external speech. It is called external in the sense of being thought manifested externally through sound. This is never for a moment apart from the motor activity of the sound producing organs. In terms of our martial arts concepts, this is an activity of consciousness in which conscious perception and motor activity are undivided, or combined into one. The degree of coordination therein is far higher than the degree of coordination between consciousness and motor activity occurring in physical exercise.

Nevertheless, when we are speaking in the course of everyday interaction, we are scarcely aware, hardly conscious, of the total motor activity involved. What we feel is simply that we are carrying on a verbalized exchange of ideas. Occasionally we may even overlook the verbalization, and feel that we are engaged in a direct interchange of thoughts, without concentrating on grammar, phraseology, vocabulary, and so on. When advanced martial artists box, their subjective feeling is also like this; it seems to be a direct interchange of thought, without concentration on power, energy, stance, or technique.

It is only when people such as performers, broadcasters, singers, or cantors are in the process of revising established articulation habits, when they are engaged in training specialist techniques of formal diction and pronunciation, that they rethink and renew their conscious perception of this motor activity. When people study foreign languages, or when they suffer afflictions of the voice-producing organs causing impediments or obstructions, they also reexperience this motor activity to different degrees. This makes it clear that under conditions of thorough development and a high degree of automatic response, motor activity shifts from manifest consciousness into the domain of the subconscious. Only when difficulty in speaking arises does it "float up" into self-aware consciousness.

This is external speech. Communication by writing is also a form of external speech. What we want to explain is that because of psychophysical coordination in the consciousness of martial arts, the motor activity involved is always sensed in the mind of the martial artist simply as an act of will, a direct exchange of thought, with muscular strength no longer an object of attention.

When external speech is internalized, it is then unspoken "internal speech," which is our verbal thinking. Internal speech makes no sound; it is no longer speech to make others hear, but rather a communication with oneself, taking place within the brain of the individual. It is individual, noninteractive intellectual activity. But even though no sound is produced, it has been ascertained by modern scientific work that this sort of activity still involves, under most conditions (such as thinking over problems, writing, reading, listening to others talk, etc.), extremely faint and relatively undeveloped muscular "pronunciation" activity. The degree to which this occurs is such that it is sometimes hidden and sometimes evident. When people write essays or copy writings, if they pay close attention they will discover that just before or at the same time as they write each word, their tongues move very subtly, soundlessly "pronouncing" the word.

The speed of internal speech is so rapid that it can coordinate with thought. There are many levels of development of internal speech. The faster thinking is, the less internal speech is developed; the motor activity and degree of faintness of pronunciation correspond to the speed of internal speech. The training of athletic expression in modern physical education is also built upon an analogous body-mind mechanism.

Once internal and external speech begin, they proceed to interchange with each other. From childhood onward, they take shape through a complex process of internalization of external speech and externalization of internal speech, repeated over and over again, countless times. The stages and levels therein are also extremely complicated, presenting endless vistas as a domain of research. A certain degree of coordination between the activity of thought and the motor activity of the organs of speech has, however, already been fully researched and fully ascertained. This fact, furthermore, also provides us with a frame of reference for research on the possibility of a higher level of cooperation, even perfect coordination, between thought and the human musculature.

Nonetheless, no matter how valuable the example provided by the relationship between internal and external speech, it is still not sufficiently complete. Practically speaking, the subtle muscular movements involved are just byproducts accompanying the activity of formless thought. In martial arts, however, these very subtle movements are one of the points of departure in refinement of consciousness; they are also an important point of attentive training in the process of refinement of consciousness. This is what "consciousness" is; this is the union of intent and motor activity in consciousness, forming the physical and mental foundation for dynamic thought.

Dynamic Thought

We can also liken the movement of the human body to the interchange between internal and external body language. However, with the smallest unit of movement, which is an action of the human body based on conditioned reflex, there is no way to form the coordination of thought and motor activity in the power of "speech." Only after overcoming the drawbacks of conditioned reflex, only with a firm foundation of consciousness in which mind and body are coordinated, does it become possible for people to establish dynamic thought. Only thus can the human body arrive at a level of action where the internal and the external are coordinated to an equal or greater degree than in the relationship between internal and external language and speech.

Once there is dynamic thought, the outer part of the human body develops fluent movement, corresponding to external language or voiced speech. Individual outward pugilistic practice corresponds to individual recitation; paired practice of offense and defense corresponds to conversation. The internal activity of the "mental boxing" (within the action of thought, which is of extremely high frequency and not outwardly manifest) corresponds to internal language, or unspoken speech. Individual boxing practice in the mind (mental boxing) corresponds to silent recitation of poetry, while mental paired practice of offense and defense corresponds to silent conversation. These activities of thought, furthermore, are accompanied by subtle coordinated motor activity in the body according to the different levels of practical attainment.

In martial arts training, these subtle movements are made into an important focus of strengthening training, making them perceptible and recognizable, susceptible to processing, systematization, and consistent linking, creating realistic forms of exercises much more substantial than ordinary training in athletic expression. In this way, martial arts create a solid perceptible and recognizable material foundation for perfectly pure dynamic thought. This is the first basis for the mode of conduction known as psychophysical coordination, passing right through the joints.

Ordinary athletic expression, which comes along with subtle motor activity associated with thinking activity connected with exercise or physical movement, has two fatal weaknesses. The first is that it is based on conditioned reflexes, and therefore remains noncoordinated in that consciousness and the body alternate. The second is that ordinary athletic expression is extraordinarily fragile; as soon as the body starts moving, the expression is easily spoiled. The purpose of training in expression is to form an ideal movement in thought, then to use this to arrive at an idealization of movement itself. However, due to the aforementioned two weaknesses, this ideal model is easily deranged and spoiled by the crudeness and coarseness of actual physical movement.

Once there is this solid foundation of consciousness, plus the ability to project it beyond the body, forming a "consciousness field" outside the body, with the ability to deliver feedback to the physical form through this extracorporeal consciousness field, so as to develop control over the physical form, then the capacity and condition of dynamic thought have undergone a change in character. Dynamic thought has the capacity to form an ideal model of physical movement outside the body, with this model having absolute dominance and power of control over physical movement.

The model created by dynamic thought, and any activity of dynamic thought, can not only produce expression of coordinated movement in the human body that is not outwardly expressed, it can also operate ideal movement that is fully manifest outwardly. This is the total process of "movement beginning within and manifesting form outwardly." Here, "within" refers to dynamic thought, which is the thought in the brain and the coordinate consciousness field outside the body. Here, the "outside" takes on expression under the control of the consciousness field to begin the activation of physical movement. This too is coordinate with dynamic thought.

In linguistic activity, external speech follows internal speech; that is to say, it follows the function of thought. In martial arts, the movement of the external bodily form follows dynamic thought, or the function of the extracorporeal consciousness field. Only at this point is the advanced exercise unique to martial arts evident: the action of consciousness produces field movement, which bring with it physical movement; all three, furthermore, are coordinated.

According to the theory of *Taijiquan*, "first consciousness moves, then power moves" (and then the physical body moves); this indicates the subordination in the relationship among the three elements in dynamic thought, but this is not the order that occurs when going into action. Of course, after the capacity of coordination is developed, one can also deliberately give the appearance of uncoordination in order to deceive an opponent. This is uncoordination that is based on the capacity of coordination, which has even more amazing power.

Beyond this, when you have reached the level of "no conscious intent," or when you have reached the level of the "original mind," then the work of dynamic thought is done. This is finally the realm where "it is so vast there is nothing outside, so minute there is no inside," "doing everything without doing anything."

Dynamic Thought Constitutes a Specific Type of Thinking

If the raw material of logical thought is concepts, and the raw material of symbolic thought is sound and form, then the raw material of dynamic thought is power freed from form and detached from images.

Let us review some of the details of the theory of martial arts. "First seek to unfold, then seek to tighten up." Tightening up does not just refer to making your motions small; it also refers to entering right into dynamic thought. There is also, furthermore, a distinction between unfolding and tightening up within dynamic thought itself. "When the refinement of pugilism is consummate, even that which is most small is still a sphere." This is infinite minuteness, so small there is no inside. "Just go from form to formlessness," "form returns to tracelessness." Formless and tracelessness mean the body is not moving, only dynamic thought is moving; and when you reach the level of the original mind, then dynamic thought itself no longer has any forms or images. "No form, no image" means that the physical form is not evident; it also means that there is no form or image in dynamic thought either.

Dynamic thought fulfills the conditions that qualify it to be considered a type of thinking. That is to say, it has the same nature as thought as a whole, as well as other specific modes of thought. Dynamic thought has its special power of generalization, which is the most universal power of abstraction and generalization. This is not a logical concept of power, however; it is a formless power preserving the sensitivity and dynamic effect of power. There is an inevitable indirectness, but it can exert effects on phenomena that do not directly act on the senses.

In other words, dynamic thought has its own independent nature, and it can be used as an independent instrument to act upon practical application, in the sense of guiding practical application. It has its own unique abstract representational logic, so it is able to react to the higher level dynamic relationships in physical movement, as well as to the regularity of changes in the objective environment. At the same time, it has its own purposefulness and a unique capacity for solving problems.

Confronting new purposes and new problems in the domain of biodynamics, dynamic thought is able to provide solutions by its own methods. Employing the modality of dynamic thought (the modality of simultaneous use of body and mind), it can present problems, clarify problems, present hypotheses, test hypotheses, and so on. Dynamic thought is layered, or multitiered, and it also has a unique productivity; it does not just passively reflect reality, but is the capacity to actively reconstruct reality.

Combining the philosophical basis and methodology of martial arts, furthermore, dynamic thought is able, by means of its special capacity of response, to discover and recognize latent physical and mental powers, as well as human auras and all sorts of energy fields in the environment that are inaccessible to ordinary modes of thought.

Without a doubt, when considered as a kind of latent capacity of the human body and mind that can only be developed by martial arts, dynamic thought is one of the greater contributions of martial arts to the science of human movement, to the whole science of the human body, and to the science of thought. The course and methodology of this particular development contain extremely important lessons for the awakening of other latent capacities of the human body.

Higher Apperception of Movement

Ordinary apperception of movement is developed when motor skills go through self-conscious training until they arrive at the point where they become automatic, after which they shift into the subconscious and combine with the instinctual, subconscious, and other motor mechanisms of overall response. Being established on the basis of training of conditioned response, however, ordinary apperception of movement cannot produce the power to leave the physical body and detach from form; therefore it cannot completely eliminate the various contradictions between manifest consciousness, the subconscious, and the instincts. Thus it cannot arrive at the level of coordination of the function of these three.

Dynamic thought, in contrast, is a product of advanced training in self-control in which the human body and mind go through a multitiered process of total refinement of consciousness. Dynamic thought is thus capable of enabling people to reach a level of profound interpenetration and harmonious merging of instinct, the subconscious, and manifest consciousness. Its highest goal is the total coordination of mental and physical activity; the focus of its training is also the development of this power of coordination. What is gradually elevated step by step in each stage of the process of its training is the degree and range of this coordination.

Ordinary apperception of movement comprises only a few particular levels among the various distinct levels of physical and mental activity, whereas dynamic thought is a process going from "doing" to "nondoing" (by which anything may be done). The advanced stages of dynamic thought already manifest this in eliminating the instinctive tension in response to attack, causing it to turn into a highly relaxed and stable condition of body and mind.

From this, there occurs a transformation of the individual's sense of self-defense. Combined with movement totally coordinated with the mental movement of adversaries, this enables the individual to be both hard and soft, to master movement by stillness, and to overcome the adamant by means of flexibility. Thus a number of pointed questions raised by modern sciences of body and mind are resolved on a transcendent level.

But dynamic thought itself is still not the goal. When dynamic thought is developed to a high level, it can also produce substantive change, so that one arrives at the extinction of the personal ego and enters into the stage of complete higher apperception. Thus higher apperception is "the original mind," "the infinite," "the void," "the Tao." Attainment of higher apperception is attainment of the Tao. Then one becomes an embodiment of the Tao, or what the ancients used to call a "sage."

In dealing with religious vocabulary, we should not take a paranoid attitude. We need to study the real, nonreligious meanings underlying these terms, using the combined intelligence and perception of past and present. In particular, there are certain terms found in Chinese classical and medical literature, such as "real human," "perfected human," and "sanctified human," "spiritual immortal," "earth immortal," "celestial immortal," and so on, that really do not refer to supreme gods or spirits in a religious sense, but to living human beings who have accomplished cultivation of nature; they simply represent different levels of advanced work on essence and life.

CHAPTER 10

Refinement of Consciousness and Health

THERE ARE SOME types of martial arts that are of a fairly high level in terms of pugilistic power, and whose training produces results fairly rapidly, yet which in the long run are damaging, even deadly, to physical and mental health. The purpose of training in these martial arts is not to foster health, but for various other short-term benefits. Deriving from historical causes and certain demands of human society, this type of martial arts may have some value, and may have attracted many young people, but we cannot classify this type of martial art as advanced or higher martial art.

The essence of martial arts theory and practical experience indicate to us that higher martial arts must be in accord with advanced medical science. Any technical principles and methods of practice lacking means of correctly promoting physical and mental health, having no way to extend life, but instead causing damage to health, are all said to be unorthodox in the theory of martial arts energetics. Even if some of those methods of training can demonstrate remarkable short-term effects, on the whole they are not worth taking up. Just like taking up the command of an army under the influence of a harmful drug or stimulant, methods that are not beneficial to health, and even possibly harmful, should not be taken up at all.

The various methods of modulating capacity and prolonging effect in various deliberate ways, such as exemplified by the modulation of capacity illustrated in our chapter on refinement of consciousness, are the principles of health maintenance common to higher martial arts.

Modulation of Capacity as Prerequisite for Health and Long Life

There are many theories of physical education and healing through martial arts; all of them take up authoritative indications and powerful proofs that promotion of metabolism in the human body, causing metabolism to take place with maximum vigor, should cause enhancement of physical health and extension of the life span. In our view, this is a biased opinion that can easily lead to self-deception.

The number of divisions through which brain cells go in one human lifetime are limited. In this sense, the faster and more abundantly cell division occurs, the shorter the life span will be. When the fuel is limited, the more intense the fire and the more quickly it will burn out. Here it will be more scientific to adopt the expression "improvement of metabolic function" or "improvement of metabolic conditions." Because metabolism and regeneration can become inefficient, so that "sometimes the fire is high, sometimes it nearly goes out," it is necessary to tune and improve it.

Modulation of capacity by refinement of consciousness, "raising little funding but getting a lot accomplished," is a deliberate method of fostering health that has long-term effects. Correct refinement of consciousness eliminates all unnecessary and unreasonable expenditure of vital energy, all physical and mental waste; under the premises of guaranteeing a plenitude of energy for living and working, and perfecting the capacity for self-preservation, refinement of consciousness lessens the speed of metabolism in a rational manner. This is the real health maintenance teaching of higher martial arts.

Thus metabolism is slowed down and stabilized, while at the same time the efficiency of physical and mental work is increased. This is an indication of the value of martial arts, their ability to preserve health and long life. If one wanted to obtain similar effects from medicinal drugs, it would be relatively difficult, and also economically unfeasible. In this respect, refinement of consciousness by martial arts, and its capacity modulating effect, are irreplaceable.

Future studies in human physiology and health can investigate the capacity modulation mechanism of refinement of consciousness through martial arts from many angles, such as biology, biochemistry, and psychology, thus to help martial arts develop even more effective methods, so as to compress the training process and accelerate the speed of training. We must not forget, however, that refinement of consciousness through martial arts, and the resulting effect of modulation of capacity, are not products of modern science. Only by respecting the traditional methods and principles of martial arts themselves, adapting scientific methods appropriately, will it be possible to minimize twists and turns in future scientific research.

Life-Extension Is Possible Only by Harmonization of Body and Mind

The ailment of humanity today, which grows ever more serious, is inner disharmony between body and mind. The great majority of diseases are produced by lack of harmony between the various levels of body and mind. Improvement of the environment is of course important, but when environmental conditions are beyond human control, the only practical thing to do is to change the ability of humanity itself to adapt to the environment.

Refinement of consciousness by martial arts requires one to go through simultaneous mental and physical refinement to solve the problem of kinetic balance of physical and mental activities, the problem of psychophysical coordination. In other words, the two major issues of biological health and psychological health should be considered a single issue to be resolved at the same time, thus enabling people to arrive at a total harmony between self and the external world.

What medicine is there, what therapy is there, that can enable humanity to resolve such a vast problem on a large scale? We say that there is no such thing in principle, nor can there be. People have to learn to address their expectations to themselves first, to place their hopes in their own ability to use their own latent powers to resolve health problems, then proceed to tune and activate this capacity in order to actually achieve solutions to problems. As it is said, "God is in your heart," and "You yourself are Buddha." The underlying meaning of these religious doctrines is that one must save oneself.

Martial arts are not, of course, the one and only way to solve problems; but martial arts have provided a brilliant example of resolution of these types of problems. The reason for this is that once you have been through refinement of consciousness like that of martial arts, you have resolved internal biological afflictions, both evident and latent; you have resolved psychological contradictions, which are the contradictions between manifest consciousness, the subconscious, and instinctive response; you have resolved the contradictions between psychology and biology, which is to have realized a total harmony and kinetic balance between yourself and the outside world (including nature and society). At the same time, you will naturally resolve the problem of capacity modulation at a high level. This is to have arrived at the aim of long life.

State of Mind and Longevity

As everyone knows, the greatest hygiene is psychological hygiene. We continue to emphasize, nevertheless, the indivisibility of body and mind; thus we call it body-mind hygiene.

The question of whether or not people are accustomed to using their own adaptivity is ultimately a matter of various objective causes. Doubt disappears through habituation. Under many conditions, however, the state of the objective world is not under our control; to emphasize objectivity then makes us into slaves of the world, and the question of our adaptivity or otherwise is controlled by that.

In reality, there is a dialectic process from uncontrollability to controllability. First we have to learn to set aside all things that are not under our personal control, so as to work on those things that *can* be brought under our own personal control. Only thus is it possible to create the conditions whereby things that are not under our personal control can be transformed so that they come under our control.

When the objective external world is not under our control, the only thing left under our control is our self. When the objective external world is under our control, it is still necessary to employ our own effort to use the objective conditions that are under our control in order to solve problems. Therefore, regardless of whether it is the internal or the external, it is in any case necessary to start from oneself in order to be able to attain a state that is under one's own control. This state under your own control, furthermore, can also be called a well adapted state.

The process of refinement of consciousness lays emphasis on self-knowledge as the basis of knowing others; only when you know yourself can you actually know others. Only when you have tuned yourself and strengthened your own ability to maintain balance in motion, can you respond to (that is, dissolve) imbalance brought on by opponents.

To tune the self means to tune the relationship between your own body and mind, to tune the relationship between subject and object in such a way as to promote coordination. The method is to lay hold of nature itself in the process of adapting to nature. If you maintain this path of training for a long time, it cannot but be reflected in your way of thinking, leading to changes in your way of thinking that enable you to learn to grasp on your own whether or not you yourself are in an adaptive state of mind. Thus you change from the "merrymaking self" into the "host of the merriment." Only such an individual can escape from a condition of slavish dependence on the objective world, learn how to master the objective world by adapting to it, and thus arrive at a state of adaptive harmony wherever one may be.

The process of martial arts training itself, leading people into higher states, can bring the student immense psychological satisfaction with each new level of attainment, each breakthrough of a physical and/or mental barrier. For this reason, whoever enters into this study usually pursues a lifelong quest for the highest state; and one achieves more the older one gets. The successive levels of break-through made in the course of this quest enable people to continually experience an indescribable psychological satisfaction and happiness. The feeling of mental harmony and self-confidence in the ability to overcome opponents and seize victory (opponents being one's own physical and mental barriers as well as the obstacles presented by the external world) gradually develop into a sort of new "habit," which is not consciously perceived even by oneself. What is more, a transformation takes place in the physical and mental state, enabling one to attain a sense of harmony at all times and in all events; and this is actually a real harmony. That things formerly impossible become possible through physical and mental health is a comparatively shallow principle.

Once this effect has been attained, what psychological afflictions are left in you? In the individual who has dropped afflictive psychological habits, vital energy is liberated from expenditure on its own contradictions, freed to pursue meaningful activity. Add to this the exponentially increased capacity unleashed by dynamic thought and higher apperception, and how could one fail to act for the welfare of the individual and the human race?

A harmonious human society can only be made by harmonious people. Thus, the more ways there are of reconstituting the human body and mind as do advanced martial arts and their refinement of consciousness, the more people can be reconstituted. Thus the contemporary malaise of the whole of modern human society could be "cured" with astonishing efficacy.

CHAPTER 11

Refinement of Consciousness and the Training of Human Character

Pugilism Is Not the Aim

REFINEMENT OF CONSCIOUSNESS is the core of higher training in martial arts. What is developed is an astounding power to kill and maim; therefore the first training of human character in martial arts is the development of martial virtues. The problem that concerns people is this: how can killing and maiming be reconciled with morality? Of course, no matter how particular we may be about "martial virtue," what martial arts develop is unlimited striking power; is it not true that martial virtue can only inhibit that to a certain extent?

We say that this is a lower understanding of martial virtue, which is here taken in a narrow sense. True martial virtue is the highest morality; on reaching the highest level of virtue, furthermore, it is possible to eliminate this frightening word "martial." The only reason we make a point of "martial" virtue is because here it is necessary to go through the course of martial arts in order to get to the highest morality.

Advanced martial artists before us have left this maxim: "pugilism is a minor art." The aim of pugilism in martial arts is "seeking the Tao." This makes it clear that in the theory and practice of advanced martial arts there is already manifest a transformation, from having fighting as one's motive and aim, based on the instinct of self-defense, to having spiritual need one's motive and seeking the Tao one's aim. On this new path, pugilism has changed from an aim to a method of seeking the Tao.

Why practice pugilism if you're not going to hit anyone? We do not promote any sort of fighting technique. We only emphasize martial arts pugilism because in the fighting techniques of martial arts there are concrete manifestations of the philosophical principles of the Chinese classics, and because they are effective methods of developing the latent physical and mental capacities of the human body, perfecting dynamic thought and higher apperception. They are also a means of pursuing the highest morality through martial arts.

The reason why morality is ceaselessly emphasized before one has reached the highest level of morality is that people who cultivate the martial still lack virtue in comparison to the standards of the highest morality, and because the highest morality is the quintessential standard of progress for martial artists. Even at the intermediate levels, the pugilistic principles and moral principles of martial arts have already been united.

Martial arts do not emphasize aggressive initiative. That is not just because of the demands of moral principle, but also because the pugilistic principle of martial arts noted earlier demands that "you do not make a move as long as your opponent has not made a move," and "be the last to act." In order to practice these principles, students in the course of practicing martial arts must first of all abandon the intention to strike others as soon as they can, turning their attention to the work itself. It is even necessary to transmute the physical and mental tension of the self-preservation instinct coming from response to stimulus. This means that in higher martial arts the technical and theoretical directions taken in the foundation work are in intimate accord with the moral direction.

Here, the instinct and consciousness associated with aggressive initiative have already been subjected to moral control as well as technical and theoretical control. What can be attained by security measures in the advanced technique of "the last to set out being the first to land," whereby one abandons the motive and intention of striking people, making the whole body and mind completely relaxed and at ease. This in itself forms part of the content of the training involved in the foundation work. In this sense, someone who wants to strike another has not reached the highest level of martial arts. And herein, furthermore, lies the key to why people ultimately need to eliminate the motivation and the idea of striking others.

Because people who have reached the highest levels of martial arts have undergone long-term transformational training, they no longer think of hitting anyone. They have already recognized the higher value of martial arts, far transcending the sense of fighting technique; thus they have recognized that pugilism is a minor art. No one with intelligence or wisdom abandons the higher meaning of martial arts in favor of fighting technique to strike others; the higher meaning includes all the noble values of unlimited richness that the principles of pugilistic technique can evoke.

Does self-defense not demand that one strike others? Self-defense that cannot avoid hitting and hurting people is an expression of martial art that is still not at a sufficiently high level. The highest aim of martial arts using fighting techniques is to "defeat the enemy without doing battle." At the highest level, no one can even pick a fight with you. The effects of the highest techniques and principles are completely consonant with the highest morality.

Basic human instincts are not completely fixed and unchangeable. Through the development and progress of human civilization, human activities whose purpose is to satisfy instincts have evolved and will continue to evolve. Activity motivated by search for the highest spiritual state and activity motivated by the fulfillment of desires are thoroughly different.

The Highest Aim of Martial Arts Is the Training of Human Character

The reason why martial arts require refinement of consciousness is that they use fighting techniques as methods of complete realization (or restoration) of the "original mind" or the "mind of Tao." It is only through the practice of martial arts, furthermore, and the practice of refinement of consciousness, that it is possible to attain this aim.

In the fifth section of this book, we explained that the domain of refinement of consciousness in its broad sense refers to the use of the procedures and methods of martial arts to practice a kind of training in which body and mind are indivisible, affecting the totality of one's own consciousness, psychology, and cultural conditioning. It refers to the discovery and development of the latent capacities of the human body and brain. It refers to the formation of character, morality, and the best of human nature. It refers to the experiential philosophy of simultaneous awakening of body and mind. It refers to the formation of a new world view, the highest level of virtue, and the highest realm of the spirit.

Here we may well use a technical term from Western psychology; we might say that what martial arts seek to produce is the individual whose "real self" is actualized in the peak experience of human life.

A small number of such people, however, is not all that meaningful. Speaking in terms of the high levels needed today, we want to solve much greater problems by producing a number of people who have realized the true self, so as to arrive at the realization of the true self on the part of the whole human race.

Chinese martial arts develop dynamic thought in people through refinement of consciousness, thence to develop higher apperception. In the course of this process, it is necessary to attain unification of body and mind, a level of coordination with the natural laws of the universe. This coordination, and only this coordination, makes it possible to develop the highest human character, the highest morality, and the highest spiritual state. Only with this spiritual state is it possible to dissolve the boundaries and contradictions between public and private realms. And only with this spiritual state is it possible to benefit humankind in a manner that is truly complete and effective.

Only by relinquishing the ego can one realize the true self; only by getting rid of conscious intention can one attain true intent; only by forgetting the small self can one find the infinite self. This is the reward that refinement of consciousness will bring to the human body and mind; and this is its most valuable gift to humankind.